Back to Basics

USA is in DANGER

Ron Berger

Published by:
berger publishing
Rancho Belago, CA 92555
mail@ronberger.com
http://www.ronberger.com

berger publishing

Printed in the USA
ISBN 13 - 978-0-9799257-8-8
ISBN 10 - 0-9799257-8-9
First Printing

Library of Congress Control Number
2010919607

Ron's Other Books

The House That Ron Built

Are You Being Served Yet?

P-NUT, The Love of a Dog

"Normal" MAYDAY

Time for TEA

Growing Old is a FULL-TIME JOB

Time for MORE TEA

Time for STILL MORE TEA

One Candle at a Time

LOOking @ . . . Things in General

The REAL Change You can count on

CONTENTS

In the Beginning

Most people today have failed Common Sense 101 when the subject was first offered. All you have to do is look at where we are and where we've come from to realize that most of us get an "F" in Common Sense 101.

The "establishment" has taken over 100 years to water down our common sense and are about ready for the kill. Actually before World War II the big push started. The country was heading for war and the people were relieved that their bout with poverty would soon be over.

Not many of FDR's programs were really working and committing us to war was an easy way out of our economic troubles. People got behind the war effort and produced well beyond the thoughts of many.

There is nothing like full employment to make a country grow. And grow we did. I remember the small "factories" in my hometown working around the clock so they could produce enough for the war effort. Much money was being spent for this effort. However, the citizens were paying for a good portion of it by buying US Savings Bonds. Therefore, the country's debt was held in check by this massive effort. Maybe we could only afford a ten-cent savings stamp per week, but every cent counted.

Taking a look back, the stock market crashed in 1929 and FDR was elected in 1932 on the platform of getting the country out of the "soup" business. FDR started many "cure-all" programs with the government spending heartily. However, we still had soup lines into 1939, just two years before our entrance into the war.

FDR had started to rev up the machinery of war which put a lot of people back to work. This was being done still with his promise to keep us out of the war. Sometimes a leader has to lie to get things done.

It was good that this was happening since England & Russia badly needed our help to stop the "Blitzkrieg" of the Germans. If we hadn't developed "lend lease" we might all be speaking German.

We were taught that FDR was one of the greatest presidents ever. However, politics always came first. The people were still hungry after six years of his administration and the programs he put in place remind me of those in place today. Sort of - I'll feed you if you vote for me.

This vein of thinking rested for several years after the war, but then picked up speed in the 60's. Lyndon Johnson was a great admirer of FDR and he started programs, similar to FDR, with great gusto which added to the already slippery slide into economic disaster.

People get used to receiving something for free that they forget that "someone" had to pay for it before it could be given out freely. Now we have generations of people on the dole and won't get off.

This is part of the problem that we are now in. People were allowed to buy homes when they knew they couldn't afford them, but did so because they could. This is one of our "cases in point" for Common Sense 101.

Our country was NOT founded on the premise that government was responsible for our health and welfare.

What
Basics?

This is an article from Dr. David Kaiser. I'm sure that most of us feel the same.

David Kaiser is a respected historian whose published works have covered a broad range of topics, from European Warfare to American League Baseball. Born in 1947, the son of a diplomat, Kaiser spent his childhood in three capital cities: Washington D.C., Albany, New York, and Dakar, Senegal. He attended Harvard University, graduating there in 1969 with a B.A. in History. He then spent several years more at Harvard, gaining a PhD in history, which he obtained in 1976. He served in the Army Reserve from 1970 to 1976.

He is a professor in the Strategy and Policy Department of the United States Naval War College . He has previously taught at Carnegie Mellon, Williams College and Harvard University. Kaiser's latest book, The Road to Dallas, about the Kennedy assassination, was just published by Harvard University Press.

History Unfolding

I am a student of history. Professionally, I have written 15 books on history that have been published in six languages, and I have studied history all my life. I have come to think there is something monumentally large afoot, and I do not believe it is simply a banking crisis, or a mortgage crisis, or a credit crisis. Yes, these exist, but they are merely single facets on a very large gemstone that is only now coming into a sharper focus.

Something of historic proportions is happening. I can sense it because I know how it feels, smells, what it looks like, and how people react to it. Yes, a perfect storm may be brewing, but there is something happening within our country that has been evolving for about ten to fifteen years. The pace has dramatically quickened in the past two.

We demand and then codify into law the requirement that our banks make massive loans to people we know they can never pay back? Why?

We learned just days ago that the Federal Reserve, which has little or no real oversight by anyone, has "loaned" two trillion dollars (that is $2,000,000,000,000) over the past few months, but will not tell us to whom or why or disclose the terms. That is our money. Yours and mine. And that is three times the $700 billion we all argued about so strenuously just this past September. Who has this money? Why do they have it? Why are the terms unavailable to us? Who asked for it? Who authorized it? I thought this was a government of "we the people," who loaned our powers to our elected leaders. Apparently not.

We have spent two or more decades intentionally de-industrializing our economy. Why?

We have intentionally dumbed down our schools, ignored our history, and no longer teach our founding documents, why we are exceptional, and why we are worth preserving. Students by and large cannot write, think critically, read, or articulate. Parents are not revolting, teachers are not picketing, school boards continue to back mediocrity. Why?

We have now established the precedent of protesting every close election (violently in California over a proposition that is so controversial that it simply wants marriage to remain defined as between one man and one woman. Did you ever think such a thing possible just a decade ago?) We have corrupted our sacred political process by allowing unelected judges to write laws that radically change our way of life, and then mainstream Marxist groups like ACORN and others to turn our voting system into a banana republic. To what purpose?

Now our mortgage industry is collapsing, housing prices are in free fall, major industries are failing, our banking system is on the verge of collapse, social security is nearly bankrupt, as is Medicare and our entire government. Our education system is worse than a joke (I teach college and I know precisely what I am talking about) - the list is staggering in its length, breadth, and depth. It is potentially 1929 x ten...and we are at war with an enemy we cannot even name for fear of offending people of the same religion, who, in turn, cannot wait to slit the throats of your children if they have the opportunity to do so.

And finally, we have elected a man that no one really knows anything about, who has never run so much as a Dairy Queen, let alone a town as big as Wasilla, Alaska. All of his associations and alliances are with real radicals in their chosen fields of employment, and everything we learn about him, drip by drip, is unsettling if not downright scary (Surely you have heard him speak about his idea to create and fund a mandatory civilian defense force stronger than our military for use inside our borders?   No?   Oh, of course. The media would never play that for you over and over and then demand he answer it. Sarah Palin's pregnant daughter and $150,000 wardrobe are more important.)

Mr. Obama's winning platform can be boiled down to one word: CHANGE. Why?

I have never been so afraid for my country and for my children as I am now.

This man campaigned on bringing people together, something he has never, ever done in his professional life. In my assessment, Obama will divide us along philosophical lines, push us apart, and then try to realign the pieces into a new and different power structure. Change is indeed coming. And when it comes, you will never see the same nation again.

And that is only the beginning..

As a serious student of history, I thought I would never come to experience what the ordinary, moral German must have felt in the mid-1930s. In those times, the "savior" was a former smooth-talking rabble-rouser from the streets, about whom the average German knew next to nothing. What they should have known was that he was associated with groups that shouted, shoved, and pushed around people with whom they disagreed; he edged his way onto the political stage through great oratory. Conservative "losers" read it right now.

And there were the promises. Economic times were tough, people were losing jobs, and he was a great speaker. And he smiled and frowned and waved a lot. And people, even newspapers, were afraid to speak out for fear that his "brown shirts" would bully and beat them into submission. Which they did - regularly. And then, he was duly elected to office, while a full-throttled economic crisis bloomed at hand. . . the Great Depression. Slowly, but surely he seized the controls of government power, person by person, department by department, bureaucracy by bureaucracy. The children of German citizens were at first, encouraged to join a Youth Movement in his name where they were taught exactly what to think. Later, they were required to do so. No Jews of course,

How did he get people on his side? He did it by promising jobs to the jobless, money to the money-less, and rewards for the military-industrial complex. He did it by indoctrinating the children, advocating gun control, health care for all, better wages, better jobs, and promising to re-instill pride once again in the country, across Europe, and across the world. He did it with a compliant media - did you know that? And he did this all in the name of justice and . . .CHANGE And the people surely got what they voted for.

If you think I am exaggerating, look it up. It's all there in the history books.

So read your history books.   Many people of conscience objected in 1933 and were shouted down, called names, laughed at, and ridiculed. When Winston Churchill pointed out the obvious in the late 1930's while seated in the House of Lords in England (he was not yet Prime Minister), he was booed into his seat and called a crazy troublemaker. He was right, though. And the world came to regret that he was not listened to.

Do not forget that Germany was the most educated, the most cultured country in Europe. It was full of music, art, museums, hospitals, laboratories, and universities. And yet, in less than six years (a shorter time span than just two terms of the U. S. presidency) it was rounding up its own citizens, killing others, abrogating its laws, turning children against parents, and neighbors against neighbors. All with the best of intentions, of course. The road to Hell is paved with them.

As a practical thinker, one not overly prone to emotional decisions, I have a choice: I can either believe what the objective pieces of evidence tell me (even if they make me cringe with disgust); I can believe what history is shouting to me from across the chasm of seven decades; or I can hope I am wrong by closing my eyes, having another latte, and ignoring what is transpiring around me..

I choose to believe the evidence. No doubt some people will scoff at me, others laugh, or think I am foolish, naive, or both. To some degree, perhaps I am. But I have never been afraid to look people in the eye and tell them exactly what I believe-and why I believe it.

I pray I am wrong. I do not think I am. Perhaps the only hope is our vote in the next elections.

David Kaiser
Jamestown, Rhode Island
United States

This lays the foundation for this entire book. We have come to the point of (almost) no return. Only the awakening of the voting public can return us to the Constitution as the basis of our government. For the last century our government guidelines have been obscured and redone to the "progressives" tune. And now it is finally being shown so everyone (who cares) can see it and reverse it.

Under the guise of progressing with the times many of our basic guidelines have taken on a completely different meaning. Government is attempting to be everything to everybody and it wasn't designed to do that. When you attempt to give things to those that won't work for it, you are actually taking it away from someone else. This will result in the lowering of the productivity of the worker, but will not raise the ambition of the non worker.

Thomas Jefferson said it best: *"The democracy will cease to exist when you take away from those who are willing to work and give to those who would not."*

Our fore-fathers were smart enough to be able to visualize what the future might hold. They formed a constitution that was applicable to all ages. It wasn't subject to "up-dating" periodically because it was written just like the "bible". The bible works today just like it worked 2,000 years ago.

One of our problems today is that our present leaders feel they know more than our fore-fathers. They feel that they have to be progressive and keep up with the times. If they would take the time to read the constitution they would find that it is "timeless". No leader today could possibly understand how the constitution came about. We live in a world - at least the USA - that has had it "soft" for so many years that the basic feeling under which the constitution was formed has eroded away.

There are many things we shouldn't CHANGE. Switching from a Republic form of government to a Socialistic one flies In the face of stupidity.

Thousands have died to build and defend our Republic form of government and to throw it away would be sacrilegious.

Very few Presidents have acknowledged how smart some of our fore-fathers were. JFK said it perfectly when he held a dinner in the White House for a group of the brightest minds in the nation at that time. He made this statement: *"This is perhaps the assembly of the most intelligence ever to gather at one time in the White House with the exception of when Thomas Jefferson dined alone."*

For the benefit of all concerned, I have included the Declaration of Independence for your reading pleasure. I'm sure most have not read it and we should know what it says.

IN CONGRESS, JULY 4, 1776
The unanimous Declaration of the thirteen united States of America

When in the Course of human events it becomes necessary for one people to dissolve the political bands which have connected them with another and to assume among the powers of the earth, the separate and equal station to which the Laws of Nature and of Nature's God entitle them, a decent respect to the opinions of mankind requires that they should declare the causes which impel them to the separation.

We hold these truths to be self-evident, that all men are created equal, that they are endowed by their Creator with certain unalienable Rights, that among these are Life, Liberty and the pursuit of Happiness. — That to secure these rights, Governments are instituted among Men, deriving their just powers from the consent of the governed, — That whenever any Form of Government becomes destructive of these ends, it is the Right of the People to alter or to abolish it, and to institute new Government, laying its foundation on such principles and organizing its powers in such form, as to them shall seem most likely to effect their Safety and Happiness. Prudence, indeed, will dictate that Governments long established should not be changed for light and transient causes; and accordingly all experience hath shewn that mankind are more disposed to suffer, while evils are sufferable than to right themselves by abolishing the forms to which they are accustomed. But when a long train of abuses and usurpations, pursuing invariably the same Object evinces a design to reduce them under absolute Despotism, it is their right, it is their duty, to throw off such Government, and to provide new Guards for their future security. — Such has been the patient sufferance of these Colonies; and such is now the necessity which constrains them to alter their former Systems of Government. The history of the present King of Great Britain is a history of repeated injuries and usurpations, all having in direct object the establishment of an absolute Tyranny over these States. To prove this, let Facts be submitted to a candid world.

He has refused his Assent to Laws, the most wholesome and necessary for the public good.
He has forbidden his Governors to pass Laws of immediate and pressing importance, unless suspended in their operation till his Assent should be obtained; and when so suspended, he has utterly neglected to attend to them.

He has refused to pass other Laws for the accommodation of large districts of people, unless those people would relinquish the right of Representation in the Legislature, a right inestimable to them and formidable to tyrants only.
He has called together legislative bodies at places unusual, uncomfortable, and distant from the depository of their Public Records, for the sole purpose of fatiguing them into compliance with his measures.

He has dissolved Representative Houses repeatedly, for opposing with manly firmness his invasions on the rights of the people.

He has refused for a long time, after such dissolutions, to cause others to be elected, whereby the Legislative Powers, incapable of Annihilation, have returned to the People at large for their exercise; the State remaining in the mean time exposed to all the dangers of invasion from without, and convulsions within.

He has endeavored to prevent the population of these States; for that purpose obstructing the Laws for Naturalization of Foreigners; refusing to pass others to encourage their migrations hither, and raising the conditions of new Appropriations of Lands.

He has obstructed the Administration of Justice by refusing his Assent to Laws for establishing Judiciary Powers.

He has made Judges dependent on his Will alone for the tenure of their offices, and the amount and payment of their salaries.

He has erected a multitude of New Offices, and sent hither swarms of Officers to harass our people and eat out their substance.

He has kept among us, in times of peace, Standing Armies without the Consent of our legislatures.

He has affected to render the Military independent of and superior to the Civil Power.

He has combined with others to subject us to a jurisdiction foreign to our constitution, and unacknowledged by our laws; giving his Assent to their Acts of pretended Legislation:

For quartering large bodies of armed troops among us:

For protecting them, by a mock Trial from punishment for any Murders which they should commit on the Inhabitants of these States:

For cutting off our Trade with all parts of the world:

For imposing Taxes on us without our Consent:

For depriving us in many cases, of the benefit of Trial by Jury:

For transporting us beyond Seas to be tried for pretended offences:

For abolishing the free System of English Laws in a neighbouring Province, establishing therein an government, and enlarging its Boundaries so as to render it at once an example and fit instrument for introducing the same absolute rule into these Colonies for taking away our Charters, abolishing our most valuable Laws and altering fundamentally the Forms of our Governments:

For suspending our own Legislatures, and declaring themselves invested with power to legislate for us in all cases whatsoever.

He has abdicated Government here, by declaring us out of his Protection and waging War against us.

He has plundered our seas, ravaged our coasts, burnt our towns, and destroyed the lives of our people.

He is at this time transporting large Armies of foreign Mercenaries to complete the works of death, desolation, and tyranny, already begun with circumstances of Cruelty & Perfidy scarcely paralleled in the most barbarous ages, and totally unworthy the Head of a civilized nation.

He has constrained our fellow Citizens taken Captive on the high Seas to bear Arms against their Country, to become the executioners of their friends and Brethren, or to fall themselves by their Hands.

He has excited domestic insurrections amongst us, and has endeavoured to bring on the inhabitants of our frontiers, the merciless Indian Savages whose known rule of warfare, is an undistinguished destruction of all ages, sexes and conditions.

In every stage of these Oppressions We have Petitioned for Redress in the most humble terms: Our repeated Petitions have been answered only by repeated injury. A Prince, whose character is thus marked by every act which may define a Tyrant, is unfit to be the ruler of a free people.

Nor have We been wanting in attentions to our British brethren. We have warned them from time to time of attempts by their legislature to extend an unwarrantable jurisdiction over us. We have reminded them of the circumstances of our emigration and settlement here. We have appealed to their native justice and magnanimity, and we have conjured them by the ties of our common kindred to disavow these usurpations, which would inevitably interrupt our connections and correspondence. They too have been deaf to the voice of justice and of consanguinity. We must, therefore, acquiesce in the necessity, which denounces our Separation, and hold them, as we hold the rest of mankind, Enemies in War, in Peace Friends.

We, therefore, the Representatives of the united States of America, in General Congress, Assembled, appealing to the Supreme Judge of the world for the rectitude of our intentions, do, in the Name, and by

Authority of the good People of these Colonies, solemnly publish and declare, That these united Colonies are, and of Right ought to be Free and Independent States, that they are Absolved from all Allegiance to the British Crown, and that all political connection between them and the State of Great Britain, is and ought to be totally dissolved; and that as Free and Independent States, they have full Power to levy War, conclude Peace, contract Alliances, establish Commerce, and to do all other Acts and Things which Independent States may of right do. — And for the support of this Declaration, with a firm reliance on the protection of Divine Providence, we mutually pledge to each other our Lives, our Fortunes, and our sacred Honor.

— John Hancock
New Hampshire:
Josiah Bartlett, William Whipple, Matthew Thornton
Massachusetts:
John Hancock, Samuel Adams, John Adams, Robert Treat Paine, Elbridge Gerry
Rhode Island:
Stephen Hopkins, William Ellery
Connecticut:
Roger Sherman, Samuel Huntington, William Williams, Oliver Wolcott

New York:

William Floyd, Philip Livingston, Francis Lewis, Lewis Morris

New Jersey:

Richard Stockton, John Witherspoon, Francis Hopkinson, John Hart, Abraham Clark

Pennsylvania:

Robert Morris, Benjamin Rush, Benjamin Franklin, John Morton, George Clymer, James Smith, George Taylor, James Wilson, George Ross

Delaware:

Caesar Rodney, George Read, Thomas McKean

Maryland:

Samuel Chase, William Paca, Thomas Stone, Charles Carroll of Carrollton

Virginia:

George Wythe, Richard Henry Lee, Thomas Jefferson, Benjamin Harrison, Thomas Nelson, Jr., Francis Lightfoot Lee, Carter Braxton

North Carolina:

William Hooper, Joseph Hewes, John Penn

South Carolina:

Edward Rutledge, Thomas Heyward, Jr., Thomas Lynch, Jr., Arthur Middleton

Georgia:

Button Gwinnett, Lyman Hall, George Walton

Not many of us have ever read the Constitution so I have copied it for your perusal.

We the People of the United States, in Order to form a more perfect Union, establish Justice, insure domestic Tranquility, provide for the common defence, promote the general Welfare, and secure the Blessings of Liberty to ourselves and our Posterity, do ordain and establish this Constitution for the United States of America.

Article I

Section 1. All legislative Powers herein granted shall be vested in a Congress of the United States, which shall consist of a Senate and House of Representatives.

Section 2. The House of Representatives shall be composed of Members chosen every second Year by the People of the several States, and the Electors in each State shall have the Qualifications requisite for Electors of the most numerous Branch of the State Legislature.
No Person shall be a Representative who shall not have attained to the age of twenty five Years, and been seven Years a Citizen of the United States, and who shall not, when elected, be an Inhabitant of that State in which he shall be chosen.

Representatives and direct Taxes shall be apportioned among the several States which may be included within this Union, according to their respective Numbers, which shall be determined by adding to the whole Number of free Persons, including those bound to Service for a Term of Years, and excluding Indians not taxed, three fifths of all other Persons. The actual Enumeration shall be made within three Years after the first Meeting of the Congress of the United States, and within every subsequent Term of ten Years, in such Manner as they shall by Law direct. The Number of Representatives shall not exceed one for every thirty Thousand, but each State shall have at Least one Representative; and until such enumeration shall be made, the State of New Hampshire shall be entitled to chuse three, Massachusetts eight, Rhode-Island and Providence Plantations one, Connecticut five, New-York six, New Jersey four, Pennsylvania eight, Delaware one, Maryland six, Virginia ten, North Carolina five, South Carolina five, and Georgia three.

When vacancies happen in the Representation from any State, the Executive Authority thereof shall issue Writs of Election to fill such Vacancies.
The House of Representatives shall chuse their Speaker and other Officers; and shall have the sole Power of Impeachment.

Section 3. The Senate of the United States shall be composed of two Senators from each State, chosen by the Legislature thereof, for six Years; and each Senator shall have one Vote.

Immediately after they shall be assembled in Consequence of the first Election, they shall be divided as equally as may be into three Classes. The Seats of the Senators of the first Class shall be vacated at the Expiration of the second Year, of the second Class at the Expiration of the fourth Year, and the third Class at the Expiration of the sixth Year, so that one third may be chosen every second Year; and if Vacancies happen by Resignation, or otherwise, during the Recess of the Legislature of any State, the Executive thereof may make temporary Appointments until the next Meeting of the Legislature, which shall then fill such Vacancies.

No Person shall be a Senator who shall not have attained to the Age of thirty Years, and been nine Years a Citizen of the United States and who shall not, when elected, be an Inhabitant of that State for which he shall be chosen.

The Vice President of the United States shall be President of the Senate, but shall have no Vote, unless they be equally divided.

The Senate shall chuse their other Officers, and also a President pro tempore, in the Absence of the Vice

President, or when he shall exercise the Office of President of the United States.

The Senate shall have the sole Power to try all Impeachments. When sitting for that Purpose, they shall be on Oath or Affirmation. When the President of the United States is tried, the Chief Justice shall preside: And no Person shall be convicted without the Concurrence of two thirds of the Members present.

Judgment in Cases of Impeachment shall not extend further than to removal from Office, and disqualification to hold and enjoy any Office of Honor, Trust or Profit under the United States: but the Party convicted shall nevertheless be liable and subject to Indictment, Trial, Judgment and Punishment, according to Law.

Section 4. The Times, Places and Manner of holding Elections for Senators and Representatives, shall be prescribed in each State by the Legislature thereof; but the Congress may at any time by Law make or alter such Regulations, except as to the Places of chusing Senators.

The Congress shall assemble at least once in every Year, and such Meeting shall be on the first Monday in December, unless they shall by Law appoint a different Day.

Section 5. Each House shall be the Judge of the Elections, Returns and Qualifications of its own

Members, and a Majority of each shall constitute a Quorum to do Business; but a smaller Number may adjourn from day to day, and may be authorized to compel the Attendance of absent Members, in such Manner, and under such Penalties as each House may provide.

Each House may determine the Rules of its Proceedings, punish its Members for disorderly Behaviour, and, with the Concurrence of two thirds, expel a Member.

Each House shall keep a Journal of its Proceedings, and from time to time publish the same, excepting such Parts as may in their Judgment require Secrecy; and the Yeas and Nays of the Members of either House on any question shall, at the Desire of one fifth of those Present, be entered on the Journal.

Neither House, during the Session of Congress, shall, without the Consent of the other, adjourn for more than three days, nor to any other Place than that in which the two Houses shall be sitting.

Section 6. The Senators and Representatives shall receive a Compensation for their Services, to be ascertained by Law, and paid out of the Treasury of the United States. They shall in all Cases, except Treason, Felony and Breach of the Peace, be privileged from Arrest during their Attendance at the Session of their respective Houses, and in going to and returning from the same; and for any Speech or

Debate in either House, they shall not be questioned in any other Place.

No Senator or Representative shall, during the Time for which he was elected, be appointed to any civil Office under the Authority of the United States, which shall have been created, or the Emoluments whereof shall have been encreased during such time: and no Person holding any Office under the United States, shall be a Member of either House during his Continuance in Office.

Section 7. All Bills for raising Revenue shall originate in the House of Representatives; but the Senate may propose or concur with Amendments as on other Bills. Every Bill which shall have passed the House of Representatives and the Senate, shall, before it become a Law, be presented to the President of the United States; if he approve he shall sign it, but if not he shall return it, with his Objections to that House in which it shall have originated, who shall enter the Objections at large on their Journal, and proceed to reconsider it. If after such Reconsideration two thirds of that House shall agree to pass the Bill, it shall be sent, together with the Objections, to the other House, by which it shall likewise be reconsidered, and if approved by two thirds of that House, it shall become a Law. But in all such Cases the Votes of both Houses shall be determined by Yeas and Nays, and the Names of the Persons voting for and against the Bill shall be entered on the Journal of each House respectively. If any Bill shall not be returned by the President within ten Days (Sundays excepted) after it shall have been presented to him, the Same shall be a Law, in like Manner as if he had signed it, unless the Congress by their Adjournment prevent its Return, in which Case it shall not be a Law.

Every Order, Resolution, or Vote to which the Concurrence of the Senate and House of Representatives may be necessary (except on a question of Adjournment) shall be presented to the President of the United States; and before the Same shall take Effect, shall be approved by him, or being disapproved by him, shall be repassed by two thirds of the Senate and House of Representatives, according to the Rules and Limitations prescribed in the Case of a Bill.

Section 8. The Congress shall have Power To lay and collect Taxes, Duties, Imposts and Excises, to pay the Debts and provide for the common Defence and general Welfare of the United States; but all Duties, Imposts and Excises shall be uniform throughout the United States;

To borrow Money on the credit of the United States;

To regulate Commerce with foreign Nations, and among the several States, and with the Indian Tribes;

To establish an uniform Rule of Naturalization, and uniform Laws on the subject of Bankruptcies throughout the United States;

To coin Money, regulate the Value thereof, and of foreign Coin, and fix the Standard of Weights and Measures;

To provide for the Punishment of counterfeiting the Securities and current Coin of the United States;

To establish Post Offices and post Roads;

To promote the Progress of Science and useful Arts, by securing for limited Times to Authors and Inventors the exclusive Right to their respective Writings and Discoveries;

To constitute Tribunals inferior to the supreme Court;

To define and punish Piracies and Felonies committed on the high Seas, and Offences against the Law of Nations;

To declare War, grant Letters of Marque and Reprisal, and make Rules concerning Captures on Land and Water;

To raise and support Armies, but no Appropriation of Money to that Use shall be for a longer Term than two Years;

To provide and maintain a Navy;

To make Rules for the Government and Regulation of the land and naval Forces;

To provide for calling forth the Militia to execute the Laws of the Union, suppress Insurrections and repel Invasions;

To provide for organizing, arming, and disciplining, the Militia, and for governing such Part of them as may be employed in the Service of the United States, reserving to the States respectively, the Appointment of the Officers, and the Authority of training the Militia according to the discipline prescribed by Congress;

To exercise exclusive Legislation in all Cases whatsoever, over such District (not exceeding ten Miles square) as may, by Cession of particular States, and the Acceptance of Congress, become the Seat of the Government of the United States, and to exercise like Authority over all Places purchased by the Consent of the Legislature of the State in which the Same shall be, for the Erection of Forts, Magazines, Arsenals, dock-Yards, and other needful Buildings;-- And

To make all Laws which shall be necessary and proper for carrying into Execution the foregoing Powers, and all other Powers vested by this Constitution in the Government of the United States, or in any Department or Officer thereof.

Section 9. The Migration or Importation of such Persons as any of the States now existing shall think proper to admit, shall not be prohibited by the Congress prior to the Year one thousand eight hundred and eight, but a Tax or duty may be imposed on such Importation, not exceeding ten dollars for each Person.

The Privilege of the Writ of Habeas Corpus shall not be suspended, unless when in Cases of Rebellion or Invasion the public Safety may require it.

No Bill of Attainder or ex post facto Law shall be passed.

No Capitation, or other direct, Tax shall be laid, unless in Proportion to the Census or Enumeration herein before directed to be taken.

No Tax or Duty shall be laid on Articles exported from any State.

No Preference shall be given by any Regulation of Commerce or Revenue to the Ports of one State over those of another: nor shall Vessels bound to, or from, one State, be obliged to enter, clear or pay Duties in another.

No Money shall be drawn from the Treasury, but in Consequence of Appropriations made by Law; and a regular Statement and Account of Receipts and Expenditures of all public Money shall be published from time to time.

No Title of Nobility shall be granted by the United States: And no Person holding any Office of Profit or Trust under them, shall, without the Consent of the Congress, accept of any present, Emolument, Office, or Title, of any kind whatever, from any King, Prince, or foreign State.

Section 10. No State shall enter into any Treaty, Alliance, or Confederation; grant Letters of Marque and Reprisal; coin Money; emit Bills of Credit; make any Thing but gold and silver Coin a Tender in Payment of Debts; pass any Bill of Attainder, ex post facto Law, or Law impairing the Obligation of Contracts, or grant any Title of Nobility.

No State shall, without the Consent of the Congress, lay any Imposts or Duties on Imports or Exports, except what may be absolutely necessary for executing it's inspection Laws: and the net Produce of all Duties and Imposts, laid by any State on Imports or Exports, shall be for the Use of the Treasury of the United States; and all such Laws shall be subject to the Revision and Controul of the Congress.

No State shall, without the Consent of Congress, lay any Duty of Tonnage, keep Troops, or Ships of War in time of Peace, enter into any Agreement or Compact with another State, or with a foreign Power, or engage in War, unless actually invaded, or in such imminent Danger as will not admit of delay.

Article II

Section 1. The executive Power shall be vested in a President of the United States of America. He shall hold his Office during the Term of four Years, and, together with the Vice President, chosen for the same Term, be elected, as follows:

Each State shall appoint, in such Manner as the Legislature thereof may direct, a Number of Electors, equal to the whole Number of Senators and Representatives to which the State may be entitled in the Congress: but no Senator or Representative, or Person holding an Office of Trust or Profit under the United States, shall be appointed an Elector.

The Electors shall meet in their respective States, and vote by Ballot for two Persons, of whom one at least shall not be an Inhabitant of the same State with themselves. And they shall make a List of all the Persons voted for, and of the Number of Votes for each; which List they shall sign and certify, and transmit sealed to the Seat of the Government of the United States, directed to the President of the Senate. The President of the Senate shall, in the Presence of the Senate and House of Representatives, open all the Certificates, and the Votes shall then be counted. The Person having the greatest Number of Votes shall be the President, if such Number be a Majority of the whole Number of Electors appointed; and if there be more than one who have such Majority, and have an equal Number of Votes, then the House of Representatives shall immediately chuse by Ballot one of them for President; and if no Person have a Majority, then from the five highest on the List the said House shall in like Manner chuse the President. But in chusing the President, the Votes shall be taken by States, the Representation from each State having one Vote; A quorum for this Purpose shall consist of a Member or Members from two thirds of the States, and a Majority of all the States shall be necessary to a Choice. In every Case, after the Choice of the President, the Person having the greatest Number of Votes of the Electors shall be the Vice President. But if there should remain two or more who have equal Votes, the Senate shall chuse from them by Ballot the Vice President.

The Congress may determine the Time of chusing the Electors, and the Day on which they shall give their Votes; which Day shall be the same throughout the United States.

No Person except a natural born Citizen, or a Citizen of the United States, at the time of the Adoption of this Constitution, shall be eligible to the Office of President; neither shall any Person be eligible to that Office who shall not have attained to the Age of thirty five Years, and been fourteen Years a Resident within the United States.

In Case of the Removal of the President from Office, or of his Death, Resignation, or Inability to discharge the Powers and Duties of the said Office, the Same shall devolve on the Vice President, and the Congress may by Law provide for the Case of Removal, Death, Resignation or Inability, both of the President and Vice President, declaring what Officer shall then act as President, and such Officer shall act accordingly, until the Disability be removed, or a President shall be elected.

The President shall, at stated Times, receive for his Services, a Compensation, which shall neither be encreased nor diminished during the Period for which he shall have been elected, and he shall not receive within that Period any other Emolument from the United States, or any of them.

Before he enter on the Execution of his Office, he shall take the following Oath or Affirmation:--"I do solemnly swear (or affirm) that I will faithfully execute the Office of President of the United States, and will to the best of my Ability, preserve, protect and defend the Constitution of the United States."

Section 2. The President shall be Commander in Chief of the Army and Navy of the United States, and of the Militia of the several States, when called into the actual Service of the United States; he may require the Opinion, in writing, of the principal Officer in each of the executive Departments, upon any Subject relating to the Duties of their respective Offices, and he shall have Power to grant Reprieves and Pardons for Offences against the United States, except in Cases of Impeachment.

He shall have Power, by and with the Advice and Consent of the Senate, to make Treaties, provided two thirds of the Senators present concur; and he shall nominate, and by and with the Advice and Consent of the Senate, shall appoint Ambassadors, other public Ministers and Consuls, Judges of the supreme Court, and all other Officers of the United States, whose Appointments are not herein otherwise provided for, and which shall be established by Law: but the Congress may by Law vest the Appointment of such inferior Officers, as they think proper, in the President alone, in the Courts of Law, or in the Heads of Departments.

The President shall have Power to fill up all Vacancies that may happen during the Recess of the Senate, by granting Commissions which shall expire at the End of their next Session.

Section 3. He shall from time to time give to the Congress Information of the State of the Union, and recommend to their Consideration such Measures as he shall judge necessary and expedient; he may, on extraordinary Occasions, convene both Houses, or either of them, and in Case of Disagreement between them, with Respect to the Time of Adjournment, he may adjourn them to such Time as he shall think proper; he shall receive Ambassadors and other public Ministers; he shall take Care that the Laws be faithfully executed, and shall Commission all the Officers of the United States.

Section 4. The President, Vice President and all civil Officers of the United States, shall be removed from Office on Impeachment for, and Conviction of,

Treason, Bribery, or other high Crimes and Misdemeanors.

Article III

Section 1. The judicial Power of the United States, shall be vested in one supreme Court, and in such inferior Courts as the Congress may from time to time ordain and establish. The Judges, both of the supreme and inferior Courts, shall hold their Offices during good Behaviour, and shall, at stated Times, receive for their Services, a Compensation, which shall not be diminished during their Continuance in Office.

Section 2. The judicial Power shall extend to all Cases, in Law and Equity, arising under this Constitution, the Laws of the United States, and Treaties made, or which shall be made, under their Authority;--to all Cases affecting Ambassadors, other public Ministers and Consuls;--to all Cases of admiralty and maritime Jurisdiction;--to Controversies to which the United States shall be a Party;--to Controversies between two or more States;--between a State and Citizens of another State;--between Citizens of different States;--between Citizens of the same State claiming Lands under Grants of different States, and between a State, or the Citizens thereof, and foreign States, Citizens or Subjects.

In all Cases affecting Ambassadors, other public Ministers and Consuls, and those in which a State shall be Party, the supreme Court shall have original Jurisdiction. In all the other Cases before mentioned, the supreme Court shall have appellate Jurisdiction, both as to Law and Fact, with such Exceptions, and under such Regulations as the Congress shall make. The Trial of all Crimes, except in Cases of Impeachment, shall be by Jury; and such Trial shall be held in the State where the said Crimes shall have been committed; but when not committed within any State, the Trial shall be at such Place or Places as the Congress may by Law have directed.

Section 3. Treason against the United States, shall consist only in levying War against them, or in adhering to their Enemies, giving them Aid and Comfort. No Person shall be convicted of Treason unless on the Testimony of two Witnesses to the same overt Act, or on Confession in open Court.
The Congress shall have Power to declare the Punishment of Treason, but no Attainder of Treason shall work Corruption of Blood, or Forfeiture except during the Life of the Person attainted.

Article IV

Section 1. Full Faith and Credit shall be given in each State to the public Acts, Records, and judicial

Proceedings of every other State. And the Congress may by general Laws prescribe the Manner in which such Acts, Records, and Proceedings shall be proved, and the Effect thereof.

Section 2. The Citizens of each State shall be entitled to all Privileges and Immunities of Citizens in the several States.

A Person charged in any State with Treason, Felony, or other Crime, who shall flee from Justice, and be found in another State, shall on Demand of the executive Authority of the State from which he fled, be delivered up, to be removed to the State having Jurisdiction of the Crime.

No Person held to Service or Labour in one State, under the Laws thereof, escaping into another, shall, in Consequence of any Law or Regulation therein, be discharged from such Service or Labour, but shall be delivered up on Claim of the Party to whom such Service or Labour may be due.

Section 3. New States may be admitted by the Congress into this Union; but no new States shall be formed or erected within the Jurisdiction of any other State; nor any State be formed by the Junction of two or more States, or Parts of States, without the Consent of the Legislatures of the States concerned as well as of the Congress.

The Congress shall have Power to dispose of and make all needful Rules and Regulations respecting the Territory or other Property belonging to the United States; and nothing in this Constitution shall be so construed as to Prejudice any Claims of the United States, or of any particular State.

Section 4. The United States shall guarantee to every State in this Union a Republican Form of Government, and shall protect each of them against Invasion; and on Application of the Legislature, or of the Executive (when the Legislature cannot be convened) against domestic Violence.

Article V

The Congress, whenever two thirds of both Houses shall deem it necessary, shall propose Amendments to this Constitution, or, on the Application of the Legislatures of two thirds of the several States, shall call a Convention for proposing Amendments, which, in either Case, shall be valid to all Intents and Purposes, as Part of this Constitution, when ratified by the Legislatures of three fourths of the several States, or by Conventions in three fourths thereof, as the one or the other Mode of Ratification may be proposed by the Congress; Provided that no Amendment which may be made prior to the Year One thousand eight hundred and eight shall in any

Manner affect the first and fourth Clauses in the Ninth Section of the first Article; and that no State, without its Consent, shall be deprived of its equal Suffrage in the Senate.

Article VI

All Debts contracted and Engagements entered into, before the Adoption of this Constitution, shall be as valid against the United States under this Constitution, as under the Confederation.

This Constitution, and the Laws of the United States which shall be made in Pursuance thereof; and all Treaties made, or which shall be made, under the Authority of the United States, shall be the supreme Law of the Land; and the Judges in every State shall be bound thereby, any Thing in the Constitution or Laws of any State to the Contrary notwith-standing.

The Senators and Representatives before mentioned, and the Members of the several State Legislatures, and all executive and judicial Officers, both of the United States and of the several States, shall be bound by Oath or Affirmation, to support this Constitution; but no religious Test shall ever be required as a Qualification to any Office or public Trust under the United States.

Article VII

The Ratification of the Conventions of nine States, shall be sufficient for the Establishment of this Constitution between the States so ratifying the Same.

Done in Convention by the Unanimous Consent of the States present the Seventeenth Day of September in the Year of our Lord one thousand seven hundred and Eighty seven and of the Independence of the United States of America the Twelfth

In witness whereof We have hereunto subscribed our Names,

George Washington--President and deputy from Virginia

New Hampshire: John Langdon, Nicholas Gilman

Massachusetts: Nathaniel Gorham, Rufus King

Connecticut: William Samuel Johnson, Roger Sherman

New York: Alexander Hamilton

New Jersey: William Livingston, David Brearly, William Paterson, Jonathan Dayton

Pennsylvania: Benjamin Franklin, Thomas Mifflin, Robert Morris, George Clymer, Thomas FitzSimons, Jared Ingersoll, James Wilson, Gouverneur Morris

Delaware: George Read, Gunning Bedford, Jr., John Dickinson, Richard Bassett, Jacob Broom

Maryland: James McHenry, Daniel of Saint Thomas Jenifer, Daniel Carroll

Virginia: John Blair, James Madison, Jr.

North Carolina: William Blount, Richard Dobbs Spaight, Hugh Williamson
South Carolina: John Rutledge, Charles Cotesworth Pinckney, Charles Pinckney, Pierce Butler
Georgia: William Few, Abraham Baldwin

Amendments to the Constitution

Amendment1 - Freedom of Religion, Press, Expression
Amendment 2 - Right to Bear Arms
Amendment 3 - Quartering of Soldiers
Amendment 4 - Search and Seizure
Amendment 5 - Trial and Punishment, Compensation for Takings
Amendment 6 - Right to Speedy Trial, Confrontation of Witnesses
Amendment 7 - Trial by Jury in Civil Cases
Amendment 8 - Cruel and Unusual Punishment
Amendment 9 - Construction of Constitution
Amendment 10 - Powers of the States and People
Amendment 11 - Judicial Limits
Amendment12 - Choosing the President, Vice President
Amendment 13 - Slavery Abolished
Amendment 14 - Citizenship Rights
Amendment 15 - Race No Bar to Vote
Amendment 16 - Status of Income Tax Clarified
Amendment 17 - Senators Elected by Popular Vote

Amendment 18 - Liquor Abolished

Amendment 19 - Women's Suffrage

Amendment 20 - Presidential, Congressional Terms

Amendment 21 - Amendment 18 Repealed

Amendment 22 - Presidential Term Limits

Amendment23- Presidential Vote for District of Columbia

Amendment 24 - Poll Taxes Barred

Amendment25 - Presidential Disability and Succession

Amendment 26 - Voting Age Set to 18 Years

Amendment 27 - Limiting Changes to Congressional Pay

I believe that everyone should know what the constitution says. This is also the original spelling.

The Constitution is our starting point. It is the blueprint for our government to follow everyday. It was written in easily understood language, but very few have read it to say nothing about knowing what was in there.

One of the shocking revelations is that most of our elected representatives have never read it. If they had, much of today's programs and laws wouldn't be on the books. Every lawmaker puts his or her own spin on what they think is needed and after awhile they get chastised if they fail to "provide" for their constituents.

We have several generations of "free loaders" that have supped at the fountain of money for so long they now expect even more. They expect raises to keep up with the cost of living.

This entire feeling is so inbreed that the real result is a lazy, good for nothing, sucker who cries the loudest when taken to task and stops at nothing to broadcast his (hers) imaginary plight to the world. Those that squeak the loudest - get the oil.

We Americans are so benevolent that we can't stand by when someone needs help. However, we never ask if they are willing to work for the handout. How many times have you taken up the person who stands on the street corner with a sign; "will work for food"? Do you really think they will come to your house to repay your gift? If they did they would lose their spot on the street. These people would rather stand there smoking than to work. Once they get enough money, I'm sure the first place they go isn't home to their family.

Our BASICS are quite simple. Life, Liberty and the pursuit of Happiness. Happiness isn't guaranteed , but pursuing it is. This really means we have to work at this ourselves and not expect the government to do it.

The Slippery Slope to Bankruptcy

Just in case you didn't know the Federal Reserve is a private company of bankers with twelve branch banks that confiscate our money and they have been doing this for almost a hundred years,--- this time! They are not part of the United States Government. Yet today they collect hundreds of billions of dollars from American taxpayers every year.

Pay attention now, you're about to read about the biggest and most successful scam in History.

"Let me issue and control a nation's money, and I care not who writes its laws" ---Mayer Amschel Rothschild

A Little History Lesson

It was Alexander Hamilton who lobbied for the first private Federal Bank, and in 1789 Congress chartered the bank.

Thomas Jefferson was adamantly opposed to the idea of a privately owned federal bank and said " I sincerely believe the banking institutions having the issuing power of money are more dangerous to liberty than standing armies".

In 1811, under President James Madison, Vice President George Clinton broke the tied vote in congress to cast the bankers out refusing to renew the charter for the bankers. Unfortunately it was President Madison who proposed a second United States privately owned Central bank and it came into existence in 1816

However, in 1836 President Jackson, overriding Congress, closed it commenting, "The bold effort the present bank had made to control the government are but premonitions of the fate that await the American people should they be deluded into a perpetuation of this institution or the establishment of another like it." (we now have another one like it)

Andrew Jackson also said, when speaking to the bankers: "You are a den of vipers and thieves. I intend to rout you out, and by the eternal God I will rout you out."

When speaking to his closest friend, Martin Van Buren, Jackson said, "The bank, is trying to kill me, but I will kill it!" (and he did)

The first two Federal Reserve Systems lasted about 20 years each and we are now almost a hundred years into the third one.

The year is now 1913, the year after Woodrow Wilson was elected president of the United States. Prior to his election he needed financial support to pay for his campaign, so he reluctantly agreed, that if elected, he would sign the Federal Reserve Act, in return for that financial support.

In December 1913 while many members of Congress were home for Christmas, the Federal Reserve Act was rammed through Congress and was later signed by President Wilson. At a later date, Wilson admitted with remorse, when referring to the Fed. "I have unwittingly ruined my country".

Now Comes the Income Tax! !!!

We didn't have nor did we need an income tax until we got the bankers back. The income tax was only needed to pay interest to the bankers for our money that they loan to our government. Yes, you read that right, the Fed, mostly on paper and computer, creates money or pays the treasury a small printing fee for currency, and then loans this money to our government. Our taxes pay them interest on this loan that cost the FEDS virtually nothing to make, what a sweetheart of a deal they have going for them.

As of March 6, 2006, the national debt stands at 8.2 trillion dollars. The American taxpayers have paid the

FED banking system $173,875,979,369.66 in interest on that debt in just five short months, from October, 2005, through February, 2006. Since this article was written a couple of years ago the national debt has now risen to 10.7 trillion dollars, and since the economic meltdown that figure has risen dramatically and will continue to rise. The United States will never even be able to pay the interest on the loan,let alone the principle. So in actuality the Federal Reserve owns the United States and our elected officials are beholden to the bankers, not the American people. The Feds are the unseen "shadow government" , they are the ones who are governing our once great Republic. They control both houses of Congress and also the President, and no-one dare oppose them. they are all powerful because they control the money supply. No con artist or group of con artists in history has ever perpetrated a scam that even approaches the scope of this one.

According to the two volume work by Bill Benson and Red Beckman , "The Law That Never Was" the 16th amendment, which created the IRS, was never properly ratified, not even by one state! These gentlemen traveled the then 48 states to verify that fact. So in a very real sense the income tax isn't legal, as many have proclaimed, but try not paying it and see how far you get before the Feds come after you and confiscate everything you own.

Henry Ford once said "It is well enough that people of the nation do not understand our banking and monetary system, for if they did, I believe there would be a revolution before tomorrow morning".

In the nearly 100 years of the existence of the Fed, it has NEVER been audited and they don't pay income tax on the billions of dollars they take from us.

According to Congressional record the U.S. Government can buy back the FED at any time for $450 million. That's about half the amount of money we pay them daily.
Do we have the most stupid and/or the most corrupt leaders in the world, or what? It seems their # 1 concern is getting re-elected, they seem to think nothing of shirking their responsibilities to the people who elected them to their powerful prestigious high paying jobs.

Congress likes the Fed because they can spend all they want with no restraints, they just put our children, grandchildren and great-grandchildren into debt.

A Federal Reserve note is just what it looks like, it's just a piece of paper with no backing whatsoever. This is why Congress hates gold and silver backed money, it forces them to live within their means. Of course they also get other perks from the Fed. perks far too numerous to mention here.

Article 1, section 8, of the Constitution reads:
The Congress shall have the Power.....To coin Money, regulate the Value thereof,....
Nowhere in that document does it give Congress the authority to delegate this responsibility to anyone, much less a bunch of private bankers.

It may be that you were never a big fan of John F. Kennedy, but you may see him in a different light after you learn how he took on the FEDS. He had the foresight to see what a bad deal had been struck in the creation of the Federal Reserve. He also had the courage to do something about it.which unfortunately, may have cost him his life.
On June 4, 1963, President Kennedy signed a Presidential decree, Executive Order 11110. This order virtually stripped the Federal Reserve Bank of its power to loan money to the United States Government at interest. President Kennedy declared the privately owned Federal Reserve Bank would soon be out of business. This order gave the Treasury Department the authority to issue silver certificates against any silver in the treasury. This executive order still stands today. In less than five months after signing that executive order President Kennedy was assassinated on November 22, 1963.

The United States Notes (silver certificates) he had issued were taken out of circulation immediately. Federal Reserve Notes continued to serve as the legal currency of this nation. It is estimated that 99% of all U.S. paper currency circulating in 1999 are Federal Reserve Notes.

Lincoln also took on the bankers and that brave bold step may also have cost him his life.

During the Civil War (from 1861-1865), President Lincoln needed money to finance the War for the North. The Bankers were going to charge him 24% to 36% interest. Lincoln was horrified and greatly distressed, and he would not think of plunging his beloved country into a debt that the country would find impossible to pay back.

So Lincoln advised Congress to pass a law authorizing the printing of full legal tender Treasury notes to pay for the War effort. Lincoln recognized the great benefits of this issue. At one point he wrote: "... (we) gave the people of this Republic the greatest blessing they have ever had - their own paper money to pay their own debts..."

The Treasury notes were printed with green ink on the back, so the people called them "Greenbacks". Lincoln had printed 400 million dollars worth of Greenbacks (the exact amount being $449,338,902), money that he delegated to be created, a debt-free and interest-free money to finance the War. It served as legal tender for all debts, public and private. He printed it, paid it to the soldiers, to the U.S. Civil Service employees, and bought supplies for the war.

Lincoln was assassinated shortly after the war and Congress revoked the Greenback Law and enacted, in its place, the National Banking Act. The national banks were to be privately owned and the national bank notes they issued were to be interest-bearing. The Act also provided that the Greenbacks should be retired from circulation as soon as they came back to the Treasury in payment of taxes.

Follow The Money!!!
When you follow the money you find there was no-one in the world who had a better reason to kill these two Presidents than the bankers. It seems inconceivable that anyone could still think there was no conspiracy in the assassination of JFK, especially when you consider the many people that were murdered or had suspicious deaths and who were associated in some way with Kennedy's assassination.

Is this proof?
NO
Is this strong circumstantial evidence?
YOU DECIDE

Concern Without Action Is A Waste Of Time!! <u>The Federal Reserve, United Nations, Council of Foreign Relations, Trilateral Commission, the Illuminati, the Bilderbergers and other elites of the hidden government are leading us into The New World Order and they are leading us fast.</u> You are not going to like it when we get all the way there, and we are over half way there now.

Only you can save this Republic!!!

The underlined portion is explained in my previous book - *"The REAL Change You can count on"*.

The Federal Reserve is not a reserve at all. They are operating under false pretenses and the Congress should dismiss them. In fact, as you have read in the Constitution, Congress has the responsibility to manage the money supply. They created this private institution to do their job.

Big money is behind all these programs in Washington. If you think for one minute that the government is really worried about your well being - guess again. They say they are concerned, but down deep you will find that politics is at the root of all evil.

THIS WILL BLOW YOUR MIND!!! You may want to invest in this bank. Looks like a winner. This is an interesting story put together from various articles and TV shows by the British Times paper. It shows what Obama and his friends are really all about. It's not hope and change, it is YOUR TAX MONEY AT WORK.....

I warn you, the first part is a little boring, but stick with it. The second part connects all the dots for you (it will open your eyes).

The end explains how Obama and all his cronies will end up as multi-billionaires. (It's definitely worth the read. You will not be disappointed).

BUT,, WHERE WILL JUSTICE BE???
A small bank in Chicago called SHORE BANK almost went bankrupt during the recession. The bank made a profit on its foreign micro-loans (see below) but had lost money in sub-prime mortgages in the US. It was facing likely closure by federal regulators. However, because the bank's executives were well-connected with members of the Obama Administration, a private rescue bailout was arranged. The bank's employees had donated money to Obama's Senate campaign. In other words, Shore Bank was too politically connected to be allowed to go under.

Shore Bank survived and invested in many "green" businesses such as solar panel manufacturing. In fact, the bank was mentioned in one of Obama's speeches during his election campaign because it subjected new business borrowers to eco-litmus tests.

Prior to becoming President, Obama sat on the board of the JOYCE FOUNDATION, a liberal charity. This foundation was originally established by Joyce Kean's family which had accumulated millions of dollars in the lumber industry. It mostly gave funds to hospitals but after her death in 1972, the foundation was taken over by radical environmentalists and social justice extremists.

This JOYCE FOUNDATION, which is rumored to have assets of 8 billion dollars, has now set up and funded, with a few partners, something called the"" CHICAGO CLIMATE EXCHANGE"", known as CXX. It will be the exchange (like the Chicago Grain Futures Market for agriculture) where Environmental Carbon Credits are traded.

Under Obama's new bill, businesses in the future will be assessed a tax on how much CO_2 they produce (their Carbon Footprint) or in other words how much they add to global warming. If a company produces less CO_2 than their allotted measured limit, they earn a Carbon Credit. This Carbon Credit can be traded on the CXX exchange. Another company, which has gone over their CO2 limit, can buy the Credit and "reduce" their footprint and tax liability. It will be like trading shares on Wall Street.

Well, it was the same JOYCE FOUNDATION, along with some other private partners and Wall Street firms that funded the bailout of Shore Bank. The foundation is now one of the major shareholders. The bank has now been designated to be the "banking arm" of the CHICAGO CLIMATE EXCHANGE (CXX). In addition, Goldman Sachs has been contracted to run the investment trading floor of the exchange.

So far so good; now the INTERESTING parts.

One Shore Bank co-founder, named Jan Piercy, was a Wellesley College roommate of Hillary Clinton. Hillary and Bill Clinton have long supported the bank and are small investors.

Another co-founder of Shore Bank, named Mary Houghton, was a friend of Obama's late mother. Obama's mother worked on foreign MICRO-LOANS for the Ford Foundation. She worked for the foundation with a guy called Geithner.

Yes, you guessed it. This man was the father of Tim Geithner, our present Treasury Secretary, who failed to pay all his taxes for two years.

Another founder of Shore Bank was Ronald Grzywinski, a cohort and close friend of Jimmy Carter.

The former Shore Bank Vice Chairman was a man called Bob Nash. He was the deputy campaign manager of Hillary Clinton's presidential bid. He also sat on the board of the Chicago Law School with Obama and Bill Ayers, the former terrorist. Nash was also a member of Obama's White House transition team.

(To jog your memories, Bill Ayers is a Professor at the University of Illinois at Chicago. He founded the Weather Underground, a radical revolutionary group that bombed buildings in the 60s and 70s. He had no remorse for those who were killed, escaped jail on a technicality, and is still an admitted Marxist).

When Obama sat on the board of the JOYCE FOUNDATION, he "funneled" thousands of charity dollars to a guy named John Ayers, who runs a dubious education fund. Yes, you guessed it. The brother of Bill Ayers, the terrorist.

Howard Stanback is a board member of Shore Bank. He is a former board chairman of the Woods Foundation. Obama and Bill Ayers, the terrorist, also sat on the board of the Woods Foundation. Stanback was formerly employed by New Kenwood Inc. a real estate development company co-owned by Tony Rezko.

(You will remember that Tony Rezko was the guy who gave Obama an amazing sweet deal on his new house. Years prior to this, the law firm of Davis, Mine, Barnhill & Galland had represented Rezko's company and helped him get more than 43 million dollars in government funding. Guess who worked as a lawyer at the firm at the time. Yes, Barack Obama).

Adele Simmons, the Director of Shore Bank, is a close friend of Valerie Jarrett, a White House senior advisor to Obama. Simmons and Jarrett also sit on the board of a dubious Chicago Civic Organization.

Van Jones sits on the board of Shore Bank and is one the marketing directors for "green" projects. He also holds a senior advisor position for black studies at Princeton University. You will remember that Mr. Van Jones was appointed by Obama in 2009 to be a Special Advisor for Green Jobs at the White House. He was forced to resign over past political activities, including the fact that he is a Marxist.

Al Gore was one of the smaller partners to originally help fund the CHICAGO CLIMATE EXCHANGE.

He also founded a company called Generation Investment Management (GIM) and registered it in London, England. GIM has close links to the UK-based Climate Exchange PLC, a holding company listed on the London Stock Exchange. This company trades Carbon Credits in Europe (just like CXX will do here) and its floor is run by Goldman Sachs.

Along with Gore, the other co-founder of GIM is Hank Paulson, the former US Treasury Secretary and former CEO of Goldman Sachs. His wife, Wendy, graduated from and is presently a Trustee of Wellesley College.

Yes, the same college that Hillary Clinton and Jan Piercy, a co-founder of Shore Bank attended. (They are all friends),AND CONNECTED!!!

Interesting? And now the closing...

Obama knows he must get the Cap-and-Trade Carbon Tax Bill passed before he loses his majority in Congress in the November elections.

Apart from Climate Change he will "sell" this bill to the public as generating tax revenue to reduce our debt.

But, it will also make it impossible for US companies to compete in world markets and drastically increase unemployment. In addition, energy prices (home utility rates) will sky rocket.

But, here's the KICKER (THE MONEY TRAIL).

If the bill passes, it is estimated that over 10 TRILLION dollars each year will be traded on the CXX exchange.

At a commission rate of only 4 percent, the exchange would earn close to 400 billion dollars to split between its owners, all Obama cronies. At a 2 percent rate, Goldman Sachs would also rake in 200 billion dollars each year.

But don't forget SHORE BANK. With 10 trillion dollars flowing though its accounts, the bank will earn close to 40 billion dollars in interest each year for its owners (more Obama cronies), without even breaking a sweat.

It is estimated Al Gore alone will probably rake in 15 billion dollars just in the first year.

Of course, Obama's "commissions" will be held in trust for him at the Joyce Foundation. They are estimated to be over 8 billion dollars by the time he leaves office in 2013, if the bill passes this year. Of course, these commissions will continue to be paid for the rest of his life.

Some financial experts think this will be the largest "scam" or "legal heist" in world history.

This makes the Mafia look like rank amateurs. They will make Bernie Madoff's fraud look like penny ante stuff.

You may want to read that again. For someone who has taken an oath and *to solemnly swear (or affirm) that he will faithfully execute the office of President of the United States, and will to the best of his ability, preserve, protect, and defend the Constitution of the United States,* he seems to be looking out for himself and all his minions.

I cannot begin to tell you how far this "cancer" has spread, but I will say that if an "operation" isn't performed real soon we will be too late to save the patient (country).

The BIG Push

After President Wilson opened the government's purse strings, FDR and LBJ expanded that practice exponentially.

FDR's New Deal attempted to fix the screw up the government started in the first place, by taking perfectly good factory workers and telling their employers that they couldn't hire them, and taking them to Montana to build fire towers instead. He forced farmers to burn crops and kill livestock, in the whacked out notion that this would raise farm prices and get the 'American Family Farm' back on it's feet. Six million pigs were sacrificed on the altar of the family farm, but no poor people got any bacon out of it.

LBJ's Great Society took money from people who worked and saved, and gave it to people who didn't have jobs and didn't want to work. Interestingly enough, the poverty rate had been DECLINING (e.g., going down) for about twenty years - then in the 60's Democrats and to a certain extent, Republicans, realized they could BUY votes with federal tax dollars. So they started every thing from subsidies to farmers to keep prices up (e.g. Milk, Butter, Cheese, Corn, Wheat, Oats, Honey, Beef, Pork, Chicken, etc..) to

AFDC and Food Stamps to help poor people pay for this food that got so expensive all of a sudden...

Yeah, I know. Sounds stupid, doesn't it. Pay farmers to burn crops and kill livestock, so family farms don't go bankrupt. Pay poor people with food stamps to buy the food. Guess who's pocket they picked to spread all this money around. If you work, but not on a farm, YOU.

Great society, eh?

During the New Deal, Franklin Roosevelt tried to promote the "progressive" view of the individual, freedom, and government's role; in his Democratic Convention Address, Roosevelt argued that "necessitous men are not free men" and that freedom therefore entailed the opportunity to make "a living decent according to the standards of the time," a definition that necessarily changes as the standards of the time change. To achieve this "freedom" in the new sense, Roosevelt wishes to wage a new "war" against the "economic royalists who allegedly jeopardize the progressive vision of freedom. In his State of the Union address, FDR more explicitly discusses the kinds of positive rights he advances: rights which "connect freedom with economic security," such as the right to a useful job, adequate earnings, decent housing, adequate medical care, and a good education.

This is a view of rights which fundamentally conflicts with the idea of negative natural rights expressed by John Locke in his Second Treatise on Civil Government. For Locke and for the Framers of the U. S. Constitution, individual rights meant that every individual should be let alone in his life, liberty, health, and possessions without positive interference by others. Furthermore, for Locke and the Framers, any claim to "positive economic rights" of the sort Roosevelt advocates amounts to positive intervention with the liberties of some men so as to provide the goods and services which are forcibly redistributed to others under the pretext that those others have a "right" to such goods and services. FDR's "positive rights" can only be implemented at the expense of Lockean negative rights.

Lyndon Johnson extended the "progressive" agenda further in his "Great Society" programs, which had as their aim the "wisdom to use our wealth to enrich and elevate our national life and to advance the quality of our American civilization." Johnson sought to use government power to transform the cities, the countryside, and the schools so as to rebuild the urban U.S. over the next 40 years, prevent pollution, overcrowding, and deforestation, and "set every mind free to scan the farthest reaches of thought and imagination"-a far cry from a limited government designed to protect life, liberty, and property.

Manifesting the "progressive" aversion to fixed and determinate roles for government, Johnson asserted that "the Great Society is not a safe harbor, resting place, final objective, or finished work. It is a thing constantly renewed..." presumably through government action. "Progressivism" thus does not recognize any end to the government's shaping of positive institutions to enable "individuality" and improve the society as the "progressives" see it. This clashes fundamentally with the Constitution's grant of explicit, limited powers to the general government and its reservation of all other powers to the people or the states via the 10th Amendment.

In their quest for expanding the role of government, both Roosevelt and Johnson explicitly flouted the Founders' desires for a highly limited role of the state in the economy and in the life of the individual. They also neglected the Constitution's protections of individual economic and personal freedoms from the reaches of government.

We, Americans, have a tendency to hold our Presidents high on the believability scale and fail to really see what's inside these political monsters. Both FDR and LBJ are peas from the same pod. Both lied and that deception led to lives being lost and the country going in debt for years to come. David Dieteman put it best when he did this study:

Many Americans today live with memories of Vietnam. Some fought there, some waited for loved ones who never returned, and some marched in the streets at home in protest. Physically or emotionally, many remain scarred to this day.

The memories of living Americans are a connection to the past, a connection stronger than mere books. This is not to disparage books; books are great. But a book is not a living, breathing person. Ask Americans about Lyndon Baines Johnson and you will likely evoke an emotional response. Love him or hate him, most Americans are not mystified by LBJ. Because they lived through his tenure, most Americans today are able to evaluate LBJ objectively.

The Gulf of Tonkin incident is widely acknowledged to have been fabricated in order to get America into the war in Vietnam. As H.R. McMaster, a retired Army officer with a PhD in History, demonstrates in his book Dereliction of Duty, the lies went far beyond Tonkin, to body counts and the fact that we were losing the war. But you get the point: Americans were sent to die because of lies.

This article is an effort to encourage Americans to reconsider two allegedly "great" presidents — FDR and Lincoln — in light of the similarities between them and LBJ.

Robert Stinnett, in his book Day of Deceit, seems to have found the smoking gun which Pearl Harbor writers such as Edward Beach (Scapegoats) and John Toland (Infamy) could only guess at: 1) official records of intercepted Japanese transmissions which prove that FDR knew of the attack on Pearl Harbor, and 2) internal Navy documents showing that Pearl Harbor was the hoped-for result of a program of harassment designed to provoke Japan into an attack.

Why all the Machiavellian maneuvers? FDR was reduced to such LBJ-like chicanery because, prior to Pearl Harbor, 80% of the American public wanted nothing to do with the war in Europe.

More than 2,000 Navy men died at Pearl Harbor, and America's 80% opposed to war swung patriotically and vengefully into war fever.

This is not to blame the American citizens who were duped by their government, nor is it to blame those who fought and died in Pacific jungles and European forests, in the skies or on the oceans. I must express nothing but gratitude and admiration for those who did their duty that others might live in safety.

This is simply to point out what was done by FDR. In The Republic, Plato referred to it as "the great lie." This is a lie which the philosopher king must tell the people so that the people may be led as they are supposed to be, i.e., so that human beings can be made to willingly act like sheep. It is so much less messy that way, so much easier for the philosopher king to get what he wants — and what he "knows" is good for people — than it is, as Napoleon did, to fire cannons into crowds rioting in the streets.

It is offensive when Nobel prize-winning economists such as the Swedish socialist, Gunnar Myrdal, refer to the mass of humanity as "cattle waiting to be led," but there is some truth to this. People are busy with their own lives, and, being generally honest, they trust politicians to act for the common good. When called upon, many men will defend their nation. Sadly, unscrupulous men posing as "leaders" often lead us astray.

Thus, despite the fact that Stinnett lays a smoking gun before his readers, he exonerates FDR for telling the lies necessary to get into the war in Europe. FDR's lies are justified, Stinnett claims, by the fact that Hitler had to be stopped, and more specifically that the concentration camps had to be stopped.

Despite the manifest evil of the National Socialist death camps, Stinnett's defense of FDR is known as "post hoc, ergo propter hoc," Latin for "after the fact, therefore because of the fact." "After we entered World War Two, we found out about the death camps, therefore we entered World War Two to shut down the Nazi death camps," is the essence of the argument.

But Stinnett's argument is contradicted by history. And such an argument cannot morally justify FDR's deception even if the lies were told solely to defeat the Nazis.

First, no one — including FDR — knew on or prior to December 7, 1941 that the National Socialists (the "Nazis") had the Final Solution in mind. Indeed, it has been argued that Hitler did not seek to implement the Final Solution until the war against the Soviet Union appeared lost.

Second, after the joint Soviet-German invasion of Poland (for which Britain and France declared war on Germany, but not the Soviet Union), the Soviets killed more Poles (400,000) than the Germans did (120,000). (These numbers come from the Museum of Communism and texts cited therein). If FDR supposedly lied about Pearl Harbor in order to stop Hitler's butchery, why did FDR ally himself with Stalin, turning a blind eye to Stalin's worse butchery?

(There is, of course, an answer to this question. Unfortunately for Stinnett, it is not an answer which can acquit FDR. Thomas Mahl's book Desperate Deception establishes that, in part, FDR was maneuvered by British agents, including those in the American press and those who manipulated other influential politicians, such as the female British agent who seduced Senator Vandenberg of Michigan — in the process turning him from an advocate of neutrality into one of FDR's war hawks. FDR was also maneuvered by Soviet spies within the American government — notably Harry Hopkins and Alger Hiss. If foreign spies can operate in Bill Clinton's White House, despite the better technology of today, is it inconceivable that FDR's low-tech White House was home to some moles?).

Third, at the Yalta conference, FDR not only allowed nations such as Poland to become slaves of the Soviet Union, he actually agreed to "repatriate" those Eastern Europeans who had fought against the Soviets. (On this point, see Julius Epstein's book Operation Keelhaul, and visit the Museum of Communism). Many Russians eagerly fought alongside the German troops on the Eastern front —

the crimes against the Russians, Ukrainians and Cossacks which the Communists had perpetrated demanded retribution. Similarly, it was the violation of Polish sovereignty which had brought Britain and France to declare war on Germany. Yet now that the war was coming to an end, Poland was not to be a sovereign nation. Instead, Poland was to be raped by the Communists. The Soviets are estimated to have shipped one million Poles to death camps in Siberia. Similar fates greeted the formerly hopeful residents of Estonia, Latvia and Lithuania. This justifies Pearl Harbor?

Fourth, if FDR lied to get into World War Two to stop Hitler, it must be considered a failure in the end, as the victory over Hitler only served to bring forty years of fear of the Soviets.

Fifth, Plato and Machiavelli aside, the end does not justify the means. Even if it is true that FDR lied about Pearl Harbor in order to "stop Hitler," it was immoral to willingly sacrifice the lives of 2,000 men in order to "stop Hitler."

It may be objected that, in warfare, it is precisely the sacrifice of lives by which the end of victory is achieved. Thus, it may be argued that FDR's decision to sacrifice the men at Pearl Harbor is no different than the decision to order an offensive which is certain to cost the lives of infantrymen. If one searches for a good analogy, where casualties among attacking troops are likely, but appear merited by a desperate situation, one might compare Pearl Harbor with Operation Market Garden.

Operation Market Garden (the subject of a book by Cornelius Ryan, and film based on the book, entitled A Bridge Too Far) was the plan of British general Montgomery to bring an early end to the war (and to stop the terrifying V-2 cruise missiles which were falling on London). The plan was to air drop the British First Airborne Division into Arnhem, in the Netherlands (nearly 70 miles behind the German lines at the time), and to race to the Dutch channel ports.

In the end, the fabled American 101st and 82nd Airborne Divisions, as well as the British Guards Armored Division, were unable to overcome the resistance of the German 10th S.S. Division. Ultimately, the remnants of the First Airborne Division snuck out of Arnhem, and Market Garden ended in failure. (As an aside, I work with two women who are related to veterans of the 101st. One woman is the child of a vet, and the other is a niece. As it turns out, the two men shared a fox hole throughout the war, and are best friends. Small world).

Had Market Garden succeeded, it would have enabled the Allies to bring supplies to the Continent more quickly (since supplies were at that time trucked up from France), perhaps ending the war by Christmas, 1944. It would also have seized the launch sites of the V-2 rockets.

Yet Market Garden failed, and the losses sustained by the First Airborne Division were horrific. Of the 10,000 British and Polish men who were dropped into Arnhem, 7578 were killed, wounded, or missing. Total Allied casualties for the nine days of Market Garden were 17,000 killed, wounded, or missing (of which 13,226 were British). This exceeds the one day total for June 6, 1944 (D-Day), with between 10,000 and 12,000 Allied casualties.

(As an aside, with reference to the earlier discussion of Operation Keelhaul — FDR's agreement to ship Eastern Europeans back into Stalin's domain — it should be noted that General Stanislaw Sosabowski, commander of the Polish airborne brigade at Arnhem, refused to return to Communist Poland at the end of the war. As Cornelius Ryan relates, "Sosabowski worked for a time in Britain as a common laborer," and died while Ryan wrote A Bridge Too Far).

This slaughter was in part due to intelligence failures by the British. German tanks were thought nonexistent due to Allied air superiority. Thus, reports of tanks in the area of Arnhem were ignored. Similarly, the low-lying polder (land reclaimed from the sea by the Dutch) was too soft for Allied armor to traverse. This confined the advance to paved roads — making it all too easy for the Germans to cut the roads, blast apart single-file columns of vehicles — and made for many Allied losses. The First Airborne was simply not equipped to hold out for as long as it took the tanks to arrive.

Was Market Garden morally justified? Insofar as it was an offensive planned on reliable information, and designed to accomplish legitimate military objections, the only conclusion can be that it was. But does the justification for Market Garden also justify Pearl Harbor? No.

Any comparison between Market Garden and Pearl Harbor misses the point of what is wrong with FDR's lying. Men will, of course, die in warfare. Mere deaths, callous as it may sound, are thus not the criterion of moral good or evil in evaluating the actions of politicians and soldiers in warfare.

To evaluate moral conduct, i.e. human action, it is necessary to evaluate a man's actions as good, bad, or morally neutral in themselves. Stinnett, taking a utilitarian line, contends that the good end (stop Hitler) justifies the evil means (lying about Pearl Harbor). This argument begs the question of whether FDR's actions were good or evil in themselves.

It matters very much that troops sent on an attack such as Market Garden know what they are doing. To let the troops know what they are doing — within the necessary limits of secrecy toward the enemy — demonstrates the respect for their lives, i.e. for their humanity, for their worth and existence as rational human beings, that is required to satisfy morality. As Immanuel Kant frames the issue, this treats the soldiers as ends-in-themselves (Kant's term for rational beings), as opposed to mere means. In other words, this treats the soldiers like soldiers instead of like bullets. You don't need to tell the bullet what you are going to do with it, but you do need to tell the man who will be firing the bullets what is going to happen to him.

The troops who participated in Market Garden knew, within reason, what they were getting into. They knew they would be opposed by German troops, although they had wrongly been told to expect less resistance than they met.

The troops who died at Pearl Harbor did not know what FDR, their commander in chief, had in store for them. FDR lied to the Navy. The troops were used as bait, to lure the Japanese into attacking, and to lure the American people into a frenzy for war.

It's a known fact that Presidents lie to the public to further their own programs. You may wish not to believe all of the above, but consider that some of these arguments have been going on for a long time and there has not been a definitive answer given. It seems impossible that there are so many stupid people in Washington that most of this information was not known or at least partially known before it really happened.

It is hard to believe that the radar on the North Shore in Hawaii showed planes coming in from the North and the big wigs believed it was the US planes coming in from the East. It's possible most of the destruction and loss of life could have been averted if the officers in charge were more responsible or our leaders more honest. We should not put our military in a position to be sitting ducks just to further a leaders program.

Back to Basics

Politically Correct

"Political correctness is a doctrine, fostered by a delusional, illogical minority, and rabidly promoted by an unscrupulous mainstream media, which holds forth the proposition that it is entirely possible to pick up a piece of shit by the clean end. "

One of the hardest things to swallow today is that everything you say is judged on whether it is "politically correct" or not. If someone judges that it's not politically correct, it casts aspersions on the entire statement. This is wrong and we need to correct this habit and get back to calling a spade - a spade. Here are some of the politically correct definitions:

Actor: metamorphosing being, possessing great wealth
Actress: metamorphosing being, possessing great wealth (and occasionally great beauty)
Android: bipedal, non-human associate, bearing immense knowledge and skill
Bag boy: agricultural product organizer
Bald: follicularly challenged
Bomb: vertically deployed antipersonnel device
Boy: oppressor-to-be
Brainwashing: cognitive accommodation
Cafeteria: dining facility
Car: earth-unfriendly, vertically-challenged mode of transport
Car Wash Worker: vehicle-appearance specialist

Cat: quadruped non-human associate
Cheating: cooperative assignment
Computer: machine bearing immense power and fallibility
Criticism: unjust self-esteem reducer

Dead: metabolically challenged
Demand: propose strongly
Derision: nontraditional praise
Dirty Old Man: sexually focused, chronologically gifted individual
Dumb: cerebrally challenged
Evil: niceness deprived
Exercise: body enhancement through exertion
Failure: non-traditional success
Fart: human ozone depletor; ecologically incorrect expression
Fat: horizontally challenged: person of substance
Garbage collector: sanitation engineer
Gas Station Attendant: petroleum transfer technician
Girl: pre-woman
Guess: anomaly maneuvers: repetitive predictions
Handicapped: physically challenged
Heroine: hero
Homeless person: residentially flexible individual
Hurricane: himmicane (non sexist)
Ignorant: factually unencumbered
Incorrect: alternative answer
Individualism: uncooperative spirit
Information: overly structured trivia
Insane: reality challenged

Kill: creating a permanent state of metabolic dormancy; servicing the target (military)
Lazy: motivationally dispossessed
Lost: locationally disadvantaged
Man: oppressor

Manhole: maintenance portal
Misunderstand: personalized interpretation
Monster: person of scales
Mugging: unforeseen funding of underclass
Murderer: termination specialist
Nerd: under-attractive, cerebrally gifted individual
Numismatist: capitalist monetary acquisition expert
Nut: hexagonal rotatable surface compression unit
Off: energy efficient
Old: chronologically gifted
Perfume: discretionary fragrance
Pervert: person engaged in nontraditional espionage
Pissed off: satisfaction deprived
Political: amorally gifted
Poor: economically marginalized
Prisoner: client of the correctional system
Prostitute: body entrepreneur
Redneck: rustically inclined
Rich: economically maximized
Secretary: stationery engineer
Sex: cooperative physical fitness
Sexist: gender biased with niceness deprived overtones
Short: altitudinally disadvantaged: vertically challenged

Sleepy: under-alert
Smart: cerebrally gifted
Specialist: physician having concentrated on a particular field of tax shelters
Structure: impersonal hindrance
Tall: vertically gifted: altitudinally endowed
Teacher: volunteer knowledge conveyor
Teaching: personality repression
Television: medium of electrons moving in disorganized patterns
Tired: rest-challenged
Uglier: over under-attractive
Ugliest: over-under-attractively gifted
Ugly: under-attractive
Unemployed: non-waged
Unsure: conceptual conflict
Waiter: waitron
Waitress: waitron
White: melanin-impoverished; member of the mutant albino genetic-recessive global minority
Woman: w/o man; woman
Zipper: interlocking slide fasteners

A way that we speak in America so we don't offend whining pussies.

Only pathetically weak people that don't have the balls to say what they feel and mean are politically correct pussies.
by Superior Intellect Oct 5, 2004

1. The laws of moral and ethical relativism; all systems of cultures and thought are equal in value, stemming from a perceived guilt from white liberals who believe that the Western Civilization is the root of all evil to the exclusion of all else.

2. A powerful form of censorship.

abbr: PC
Political correctness has a basic flaw. If all views are equal, why do some who embrace this view feel the need to push this agenda as the "correct" one at the same time demonizing other views as "incorrect"?
by tradesman Mar 31, 2003

The ideology of weird left wing liberals who want society to be nothing but accepting of all perverts and freaks everywhere. The main basis is not to offend anyone with one little incorrect word.
Jamal was offended by me calling him a perverted gay fairy black boy all stung out on crack. The politically correct thing to say would be that Jamal is leading an acceptable alternative lifestyle as an african-american homosexual who has the disease of drug addiction.
by John J. Cock Oiler Jul 26, 2003

A method of controlling and dictating public speech and thought.

Movement in America founded on well-meaning intentions to promote equality in language and representation of diverse groups. However, this has now been oversimplified and misused by politicians in their attempt to win the favor of as many "minority" and interest groups as possible.

The struggle to be "politically correct" has made common people easily irritable and oversensitive to the words of others and their own words. It has created a society that walks on eggshells and that has difficulty being personal with each other because coworkers and potential friends can't joke around for fear of offending the other.

The use of the word "American" to describe the United States is being written out of U.S. History and Government textbooks for fear of it being "politically incorrect" and offensive to South Americans and Canadians.

Quoting a friend: "Someone shouted at me today for making fun of Jews. He said it was politically incorrect. That was before he found out that I was Jewish, and making fun of ourselves is a part of Jewish culture."

Soon first-year high school and college students will be called "freshpersons" to be politically correct.
by Elizabeth Jan 15, 2005

A form of censorship practiced by faggots and leftist subversive fucks so they don't have to hear any points of view that they don't agree with. "You can't say 'George Bush'. It offends me. I have the right to not be offended" by Cardinal Mar 14, 2005

People who try so hard to say the right thing they end up just looking like twats in that kiddies program with the little purple dinosaur. There's the asian kid, the ginger kid, the african kid, the kid in the wheelchair and the big fat dinosaur.

I'm really tired of hearing all about "Black History Month, Kwanzaa, Negro Colleges, Mexican Heritage Month, Afro-Americans, Hispanics and any other "moniker" you can find. You can bet that if I wanted a "White History Month or a "White College" or a White specific anything, I would be called a racist. But those that are not white have the "right" to be heard.

This is an article by Anne Wortham. She is Associate Professor of Sociology at Illinois State University and continuing Visiting Scholar at Stanford University 's Hoover Institution.

She is a member of the American Sociological Association and the American Philosophical Association.

She has been a John M. Olin Foundation Faculty Fellow, and honored as a Distinguished Alumni of the Year by the National Association for Equal Opportunity in Higher Education.

In fall 1988 she was one of a select group of intellectuals who were featured in Bill Moyer's television series, "A World of Ideas." The transcript of her conversation with Moyers has been published in his book, A World of Ideas.

Dr. Wortham is author of "The Other Side of Racism: A Philosophical Study of Black Race Consciousness" which analyzes how race consciousness is transformed into political strategies and policy issues.

She has published numerous articles on the implications of individual rights for civil rights policy, and is currently writing a book on theories of social and cultural marginality.

Recently, she has published articles on the significance of multiculturalism and Afrocentricism in education, the politics of victimization and the social and political impact of political correctness. Shortly after an interview in 2004, she was awarded tenure.

This article by her is really, really something.

Fellow Americans,

Please know: I am Black; I grew up in the segregated South. I did not vote for Barack Obama; I wrote in Ron Paul's name as my choice for president. Most importantly, I am not race conscious. I do not require a Black president to know that I am a person of worth, and that life is worth living. I do not require a Black president to love the ideal of America.

I cannot join you in your celebration. I feel no elation. There is no smile on my face. I am not jumping with joy. There are no tears of triumph in my eyes. For such emotions and behavior to come from me, I would have to deny all that I know about the requirements of human flourishing and survival - all that I know about the history of the United States of America, all that I know about American race relations, and all that I know about Barack Obama as a politician. I would have to deny the nature of the "change" that Obama asserts has come to America .

Most importantly, I would have to abnegate my certain understanding that you have chosen to sprint down the road to serfdom that we have been on for over a century. I would have to pretend that individual liberty has no value for the success of a human life. I would have to evade your rejection of the slender reed of capitalism on which your success and mine depend. I would have to think it somehow rational that 94 percent of the 12 million Blacks in this country voted for a man because he looks like them (that Blacks are permitted to play the race card), and that they were joined by self-declared "progressive" whites who voted for him because he doesn't look like them.

I would have to wipe my mind clean of all that I know about the kind of people who have advised and taught Barack Obama and will fill posts in his administration - political intellectuals like my former colleagues at the Harvard University's Kennedy School of Government.

I would have to believe that "fairness" is equivalent of justice. I would have to believe that a man who asks me to "go forward in a new spirit of service, in a new service of sacrifice" is speaking in my interest. I would have to accept the premise of a man that economic prosperity comes from the "bottom up," and who arrogantly believes that he can will it into existence by the use of government force. I would have to admire a man who thinks the standard of living of the masses can be improved by destroying the most productive and the generators of wealth.

Finally, Americans, I would have to erase from my consciousness the scene of 125,000 screaming, crying, cheering people in Grant Park, Chicago irrationally chanting "Yes We Can!" Finally, I would have to wipe all memory of all the times I have heard politicians, pundits, journalists, editorialists, bloggers and intellectuals declare that capitalism is dead - and no one, including especially Alan Greenspan, objected to their assumption that the particular version of the anti-capitalistic mentality that they want to replace with their own version of anti-capitalism is anything remotely equivalent to capitalism.

So you have made history, Americans. You and your children have elected a Black man to the office of the president of the United States, the wounded giant of the world. The battle between John Wayne and Jane Fonda is over - and Fonda won. Eugene McCarthy and George McGovern must be very happy men. Jimmie Carter, too. And the Kennedys have at last gotten their Kennedy look-a-like. The self-righteous welfare statists in the suburbs can feel warm moments of satisfaction for having elected a Black person.

So, toast yourselves: 60s countercultural radicals, 80s yuppies and 90s bourgeois bohemians. Toast yourselves, Black America . Shout your glee Harvard, Princeton, Yale, Duke, Stanford, and Berkeley. You have elected not an individual who is qualified to be president, but a Black man who, like the pragmatist Franklin Roosevelt, promises to - Do Something! You now have someone who has picked up the baton of Lyndon Johnson's Great Society. But you have also foolishly traded your freedom and mine - what little there is left - for the chance to feel good.

There is nothing in me that can share your happy obliviousness. God Help Us all.

Please note that I have nothing against "black people" or "brown people" or any other color you can mention. I've had - and still have - many friendly relations with all colors. One of my best friends and "promoters" was a black sergeant in the Air Force. I have many neighbors that are of varying ethnic backgrounds and I am friendly with them all. They all deserve the best that this country can offer.

My only concerns are those that are lazy, expect handouts, continually holler for more and give the feeling that they are better than anyone around. Those are the ones that have explicit demands and seem to start all the "politically correct" crap that we have today.

They also need to drop the "African-American" handle they have adopted. None are from Africa and many couldn't point to it on the map. If they are here legally or born here, they are Americans - PERIOD.

A Black man's point of view.

A BLACK MAN, THE PROGRESSIVE'S PERFECT TROJAN HORSE

By Lloyd Marcus

As millions of my fellow Americans, I am outraged, devastated and extremely angry by the democrat's unbelievable arrogance and disdain for We The People. Despite our screaming "no" from the rooftops, they forced Obamacare down our throats. Please forgive me for using the following crude saying, but it is very appropriate to describe what has happened. "Don't urinate on me and tell me it's raining." Democrats say their mission is to give all Americans health care. The democrats are lying. Signing Obamacare into law against our will and the Constitution is tyranny and step one of their hideous goal of having as many Americans as possible dependent on government, thus controlling our lives and fulfilling Obama's promise to fundamentally transform America .

I keep asking myself. How did our government move so far from the normal procedures of getting things done? Could a white president have so successfully pulled off shredding the Constitution to further his agenda? I think not.

Ironically, proving America is completely the opposite of the evil racist country they relentlessly accuse her of being, progressives used   America's goodness, guilt and sense of fair play against her.. In their quest to destroy   America as we know it, progressives borrowed a brilliant scheme from Greek mythology. They offered America a modern day Trojan Horse, a beautifully crafted golden shiny new black man as a presidential candidate. Democrat Joe Biden lauded Obama as the first clean and articulate African American candidate. Democrat Harry Reid said Obama only uses a black dialect when he wants.

White America relished the opportunity to vote for a black man naively believing they would never suffer the pain of being called racist again. Black Americans viewed casting their vote for Obama as the ultimate Affirmative Action forAmerica 's sins of the past.

Then there were the entitlement loser voters who said, "I'm votin' for the black dude who promises to take from those rich SOBs and give to me."

Just as the deceived Trojans dragged the beautifully crafted Trojan Horse into Troy as a symbol of their victory, deceived Americans embraced the progressive's young, handsome, articulate and so called moderate black presidential candidate as a symbol of their liberation from accusation of being a racist nation. Also like the Trojan Horse, Obama was filled with the enemy hiding inside.

Sunday, March 21, 2010, a secret door opened in Obama, the shiny golden black man. A raging army of democrats charged out. Without mercy, they began their vicious bloody slaughter of every value, freedom and institution we Americans hold dear; launching the end of America as we know it.

Wielding swords of votes reeking with the putrid odor of back door deals, the democrats landed a severe death blow to America and individual rights by passing Obamacare.

The mainstream liberal media has been relentlessly badgering the Tea Party movement with accusations of racism. Because I am a black tea party patriot, I am bombarded with interviewers asking me the same veiled question. "Why are you siding with these white racists against America's first African American president?" I defend my fellow patriots who are white stating, "These patriots do not give a hoot about Obama's skin color. They simply love their country and oppose his radical agenda. Obama's race is not an issue."

Recently, I have come to believe that perhaps I am wrong about Obama's race not being an issue. In reality, Obama's presidency has everything to do with racism, but not from the Tea Party movement. Progressives and Obama have exploited his race from the rookie senator's virtually unchallenged presidential campaign to his unprecedented bullying of America into Obamacare. Obama's race trumped all normal media scrutiny of him as a presidential candidate and most recently even the Constitution of the United States .. Obamacare forces all Americans to purchase health care which is clearly unconstitutional.

No white president could get away with boldly and arrogantly thwarting the will of the American people and ignoring laws. President Clinton tried universal health care. Bush tried social security reform. The American people said "no" to both president's proposals and it was the end of it. So how can Obama get away with giving the American people the finger? The answer. He is black.

The mainstream liberal media continues to portray all who oppose Obama in any way as racist. Despite a list of failed policies, overreaches into the private sector, violations of the Constitution and planned destructive legislation too numerous to mention in this article, many Americans are still fearful of criticizing our first black president. Incredible.

My fellow Americans, you must not continue to allow yourselves to be "played" and intimidated by Obama's race or the historical context of his presidency. If we are to save America , the greatest nation on the planet, Obama's progressive agenda must be stopped.

Lloyd Marcus (black) Unhyphenated American, Singer/Songwriter, Entertainer, Author, Artist & Tea Party Patriot

SHARE THIS WITH AMERICA ! ! ! !

Back to Basics

Are We Falling?

No government, kingdom or society lasts forever. Here are seven factors that contributed to ancient Rome's demise-warning signs that exist today within the nations of the American and British peoples.

There are 'striking similarities' between America's current situation and the factors that brought down Rome, including 'declining moral values and political civility at home, an over-confident and over-extended military in foreign lands and fiscal irresponsibility by central government.'"

History reveals that all governments, empires and kingdoms of men, no matter how grand, no matter how powerful, ultimately fall. It happened to ancient Egypt, Assyria and Babylon. Even Rome was not exempt; though it dominated much of Europe, Northern Africa, the Middle East and parts of the Near East, and lasted for 500 years, the Roman Empire ultimately fell.

There is an old and popular saying: "Rome was not built in a day." Likewise, the Roman Empire did not fall in one night; its decline was gradual. Not long after it rose to world dominance, several factors were already at work contributing to the empire's ultimate demise. Similarly, these factors are at work among the societies of the American and British peoples-and serve as warning signs of a civilization destined to fall.

The Family Unit:

Few understand that the family unit is the basic building block of every thriving society. Within the family, young minds are first taught the importance of building character, controlling one's emotions, setting worthwhile goals, striving for excellence-or at least this should be the case, as it was generations ago.

At the start of the Roman Empire, fathers took seriously their role in properly instructing, training and educating their sons, and mothers taught their daughters as well. The example of strong and active parents daily ingrained into children the importance of obedience, deference to civic authority and respect for the laws of the land.

But as new generations came of age, the family weakened and fractured. Husbands and wives gave in to the pulls of human nature to engage in widespread adultery, inevitably leading to increasing rates of broken marriages. Divorce for virtually any reason became legal; wives only had to say to their husbands three times in succession, "I divorce you!" to bring it to pass. Also, parents came to spoil their children, who then grew up to become lazy adults who were irreverent, disobedient to authority and had little respect for the elderly or the "old paths" of social norms and values.

Likewise, the family unit in America, Britain, Australia, Canada and other sister nations of the West is under constant assault. Broken marriages and fractured households are now the norm. Few fathers exercise a strong hand in teaching, guiding and correcting their young, often leaving mothers to fill both parental roles.

Children are growing up pampered and catered to, never learning to accept and recover from setbacks-never being taught to "rise up before the hoary head, and honor the face of the old man" (Lev. 19:32), which is connected to fearing God-never instructed to think of others before themselves. They live in a fantasy world in which they "must" have cellphones; they "need" their privacy; they "have rights."

As with ancient Rome, the British and American peoples (like their forefathers, the ancient Israelites) ignore God's counsel: "Stand you in the old ways, and see, and ask for the old paths" (Jer. 6:16). The birthright nations of today respond the same way as did their forefathers, ancient Israel: "We will not walk therein" (same verse).

Modern parents believe they know better than their Creator, and thus ignore important biblical instruction such as, "The rod and reproof give wisdom: but a child left to himself brings his mother to shame" (Prov. 29:15) and "Correct your son, and he shall give you rest; yes, he shall give delight unto your soul" (vs. 17). The result? A generation of children who oppress and rule over their parents and show no respect for their elders (Isa. 3:4-5, 12).

Education:

The Roman Empire began with an educational system that emphasized developing character, morality, patriotism and social values in young lives. The goal was to develop the whole person. But this was eventually replaced by an emphasis almost exclusively on academics, with no moral or ethical absolutes defining right and wrong. Similarly, character development, patriotism and civic duty are seldom taught in the public schools of the West, where God and the Bible are banished, and morally unchecked "creative expression" is encouraged.

Because the modern house of Israel rejects God's Word, the foundation of all true knowledge, God declares, "My people are destroyed for lack of knowledge" (Hos. 4:6). He describes them as blind men groping around in spiritual darkness (Isa. 59:9-10).

Religion:

The Romans were pagan idol worshippers who took the gods of the Greeks and gave them Roman names. Accompanying the assortment of false gods was lascivious religious rituals and customs. Temple prostitution, drunkenness and other vices that appealed to the flesh were common across the empire. Similar to the Greeks, the Romans worshipped mythological figures who freely gave in to carnal desires-deceiving, stealing, getting drunk and committing fornication, adultery, even rape!

Today, millions of Americans, Britons and others claim to worship only one deity, the God of the Bible-yet their actions scream something quite different!

The word worship means to "regard with great or extravagant respect, honor, or devotion." Do the British and American peoples truly worship the God of Abraham, Isaac and Jacob? Or do their actions show they revere manmade "gods"?-celebrities who by word and example influence shallow minds to copy their irresponsible behavior. Politicians who are forgiven for reckless conduct as long they raise the banner of political correctness and "progressive" (read: permissive, radical) causes, and proudly proclaim that their personal, moral, religious or "spiritual" beliefs will never stand in the way of pleasing the masses.

Millions within America's religious community are quick to proclaim their religious fervor. But among them are those leading hypocritical lives, speaking out against sexual immorality, yet secretly engaging in it. Among priests, preachers and other prominent religionists are child molesters, closeted homosexuals and serial adulterers.

Pagan worshippers of ancient Rome sought an endless plethora of gods-but their religious beliefs were shallow, lifeless and without true meaning. Followers were left without direction, seeking spiritual purpose but never finding it.

It is the same in modern times. The hypocrisy of religious leaders has jaded millions, and their message of a God without laws-who does not hold followers to a higher standard of conduct and thinking-a "prosperity gospel" without expectations from believers-is ultimately empty. The result is a spiritual wasteland of human ideas that may sound appealing, but are not of the Bible-and has nothing to do with the true gospel (literally "good news") that Jesus Christ preached: the kingdom of God (Mark 1:14-15).

Pleasure-Seeking:

The Romans were masters of extreme pleasure-seeking. They entertained themselves with gladiators (rock stars of the day) and gambled on who would live or die. They enjoyed the sight of Christians, Jews and other enemies of the state being eaten alive by wild animals shipped from exotic regions. Residents were proud of their lavish villas, imported cuisine and fine attire. They thrilled themselves with plays, bathhouses, indoor pools and drunken parties held in the honor of Bacchus, the false god of wine and sensual pleasures.

Similarly, the modern descendants of the "lost" tribes of Israel entertain themselves, with mindless "reality" television programs driven by deception and gratuitous sex. With superstar athletes who proudly show off their tattoos and pride themselves on their multi-million-dollar contracts-yet are void of prudence, judgment and character.

Advertising, news media and Hollywood promotes materialism and covetousness. A society that loves to emulate wanton lifestyles portrayed in movies and pursue sports, gambling, theater, music and other distractions over seeking true values is destined to collapse-as did Rome.

Economy, Government and the Military:

Originally, agriculture and land ownership were Rome's chief sources of wealth-and became the most heavily taxed. Over time, landowners who operated large farms on the backs of slaves eventually undersold smaller farmers, forcing them out of business. In addition, importing foods from both conquered lands and more easily accessible distant foreign ports also began to take its toll. Commercial trade in Rome created a massive consumer economy that focused on services rather than production and growth-just as in modern-day America and Britain.

As the Roman Empire expanded, so did the costs of operating it. Rapidly growing government bureaucracy became expensive to maintain. For instance, it took an army of officials to man and work the increasingly complicated "red tape" filing system, which faced demands from both government services and the military.

To compensate for inflation, Roman emperors in the second and third centuries produced more coins, but these were no longer made of silver and gold alloys, which had become scarce. Roman currency dwindled in value. The citizenry strained under heavy tax burdens, as the government left no stone unturned in seeking potential revenue sources.

Today, Americans pay local, municipal, county, state and federal taxes before even receiving their paychecks, and contend with numerous consumer taxes: sales, gasoline, vehicles, property, licenses, pets, luxury items, airline flights-the list seems endless.

Taxes combined with inflation and a desire to maintain an unrealistic standard of living have driven a growing majority to live on credit and practice the materialistic principle of "live for today, forget about tomorrow."

Consumers survive paycheck to paycheck, partly due to wrong financial priorities and living beyond their means. A new car or home suddenly becomes a "necessity" based on the maximum amount of a "pre-qualified" bank loan, rather than actual needs. British, Canadian, Australian and American consumers are strapped with debt, resulting in a staggering number of defaulted home loans and personal bankruptcies.

As in ancient Rome, strong belief in self-determination and self-reliance has been replaced with an attitude of expecting something for nothing. Government-run systems originally intended to assist those in genuine need are now considered an entitlement.

Americans want to have their economic "cake and eat it too"-to work less and play more-to "support the troops," but have their family members and friends in the military stay home-to fight terrorism, but not raise taxes to support the military (which does the actual fighting)-to obtain better health insurance, but force employers to pay for it-to receive social security when they retire, but not increase how much they pay into it now.

Of course, how can the average consumer be expected to show fiscal responsibility when government leaders fail to do so? For example, when the Pentagon pays a small parts supplier $998,798 to ship two 19-cent washers to a U.S. Army base! Or when a Korean War veteran has to buy his own

Purple Heart at a military surplus store because the Navy informed him the medal was "out of stock"!

And just as the Roman army was overstretched and overextended in foreign lands, so is the American military. Roman soldiers, once known for their precision in battle and rigid obedience to authority, eventually became demoralized. The same can be said of U.S. troops, among whom suicide rates have risen since the start of the war in Iraq-60 in 2003, 67 in 2004, 88 in 2005 and 99 in 2006. Desperate not to return to Iraq, one soldier paid someone $500 to shoot him in the leg!

A Kingdom That Will Never Fall:

Family, education, religion, pleasure-seeking, the economy, government and the military. The failure of these and other factors have contributed to the death of men's governments-and are at work in the birthright nations of America and Britain.

However, there is a future government that will be established by a perfect Leader, as foretold in Isaiah 9: "For unto us a Child is born, unto us a Son is given: and the government shall be upon His shoulder: and His name shall be called Wonderful, Counselor, The mighty God, The everlasting Father, The Prince of Peace. Of the increase of His government and peace there shall be no end" (vs. 6-7).

An incorruptible King, Jesus Christ, will direct His government-the kingdom of God-to teach true family values; place educational institutions upon the right foundation; empower true religion to provide guidance and purpose to empty lives; maintain a global economy that will never see a depression-or even a recession; ensure that government on all levels will be free of bureaucracy; and convert all weapons to a greater purpose (Isa. 2:4).

And this world-ruling kingdom will never fall!

http://www.turnbacktogod.com/signs-of-a-falling-nation-beware-america-and-britain/#ixzz17wSgfnZf

Read more at Signs of a Falling Nation : Beware America and Britain (used with permission)

Talk about history repeating itself!

RECENT VIRGINIA CHURCH SERVICE - STIMULUS SERMON

Genesis 47:13-27

I would love to give the Pastor of this predominantly black church in Virginia a hug and a high five. This guy is obviously a leader.

Perhaps we should each decide who our real leader is.....It is amazing to see that very little has changed in 4,000 years.

Good morning, brothers and sisters; it's always a delight to see the pews crowded on Sunday morning, and so eager to get into God's Word. Turn with me in your Bibles, if you will to the 47th chapter of Genesis, we'll begin our reading at verse 13, and go through verse 27.

Brother Ray, would you stand and read that great passage for us?
.....(reading)...

Thank you for that fine reading, Brother Ray. So we see that economic hard times fell upon Egypt , and the people turned to the government of Pharaoh to deal with this for them. And Pharaoh nationalized the grain harvest, and placed the grain in great storehouses that he had built. So the people brought their money to Pharaoh, like a great tax increase, and gave it all to him willingly in return for grain. And this went on until their money ran out, and they were hungry again.

So when they went to Pharaoh after that, they brought their livestock, their cattle, their horses, their sheep, and their donkey - to barter for grain, and verse 17 says that only took them through the end of that year.

But the famine wasn't over, was it? So the next year, the people came before Pharaoh and admitted they had nothing left, except their land and their own lives. "There is nothing left in the sight of my lord but our bodies and our land. Why should we die before your eyes, both we and our land? Buy us and our land for food, and we with our land will be servants to Pharaoh." So they surrendered their homes, their land, and their real estate to Pharaoh's government, and then sold themselves into slavery to him, in return for grain.

What can we learn from this, brothers and sisters?

That turning to the government instead of to God to be our provider in hard times only leads to slavery? Yes.. That the only reason government wants to be our provider is to also become our master?

Yes.

But look how that passage ends, brothers and sisters! Thus Israel settled in the land of Egypt , in the land of Goshen . And they gained possessions in it, and were fruitful and multiplied greatly." God provided for His people, just as He always has! They didn't end up giving all their possessions to government, no, it says they gained possessions! But I also tell you a great truth today, and an ominous one.

We see the same thing happening today - the government today wants to "share the wealth" once again, to take it from us and redistribute it back to us. It wants to take control of healthcare, just as it has taken control of education, and ration it back to us, and when government rations it, then government decides who gets it, and how much, and what kind. And if we go along with it, and do it willingly, then we will wind up no differently than the people of Egypt did four thousand years ago - as slaves to the government, and as slaves to our leaders.

What Mr. Obama's government is doing now is no different from what Pharaoh's government did then, and it will end the same. And a lot of people like to call Mr.Obama a "Messiah," don't they? Is he a Messiah? A savior? Didn't the Egyptians say, after Pharaoh made them his slaves, "You have saved our lives; may it please my lord, we will be servants to Pharaoh"?

Well, I tell you this - I know the Messiah; the Messiah is a friend of mine; and Mr. OBAMA IS NO MESSIAH!

No, brothers and sisters, if Mr. Obama is a character from the Bible, then he is Pharaoh. Bow with me in prayer, if you will...

Lord, You alone are worthy to be served, and we rely on You, and You alone. We confess that the government is not our deliverer, and never rightly will be. We read in the eighth chapter of 1 Samuel, when Samuel warned the people of what a ruler would do, where it says "And in that day you will cry out because of your king, whom you have chosen for yourselves, but the LORD will not answer you in that day.."

And Lord, we acknowledge that day has come. We cry out to you because of the ruler that we have chosen for ourselves as a nation. Lord, we pray for this nation. We pray for revival, and we pray for deliverance from those who would be our masters. Give us hearts to seek You and hands to serve You, and protect Your people from the atrocities of Pharaoh's government.

New Orleans Went Under--A Black Man ' s Comments

Carefully read the whole article. You ' ll be amazed at this guy!!!

I don ' t know the man who wrote this, but I looked at his picture and read it with my mouth hanging open. He says things here that no white man could ever write and keep his job as a writer.

Say a hurricane is about to destroy the city you live in. Two questions:
What would you do?
What would you do if you were black?

Sadly, the two questions don't have the same answer.

To the first: Most of us would take our families out of that city quickly to protect them from danger. Then, able-bodied men would return to help others in need, as wives and others cared for children, elderly, infirm and the like.

For better or worse, Hurricane Katrina has told us the answer to the second question. If you're black and a hurricane is about to destroy your city, you'll probably wait for the government to save you.

This was not always the case. Prior to 40 years ago,

Ron Berger   121 such a pathetic performance by the black community in a time of crisis would have been inconceivable. The first response would have come from black men. They would take care of their families, bring them to safety, and then help the rest of the community. Then local government would come in.

No longer. When 75 percent of New Orleans residents had left the city, it was primarily immoral, welfare-pampered blacks that stayed behind and waited for the government to bail them out. This, as we know, did not turn out good results.

Enter Jesse Jackson and Louis Farrakhan. Jackson and Farrakhan laid blame on ' racist ' President Bush. Farrakhan actually proposed the idea that the government blew up a levee so as to kill blacks and save whites. The two demanded massive governmental spending to rebuild New Orleans, above and beyond the federal government's proposed $60 billion. Not only that, these two were positioning themselves as the gatekeepers to supervise the dispersion of funds. Perfect: Two of the most dishonest elite blacks in America, 'overseeing ' billions of dollars. I wonder where that money will end up.

Of course, if these two were really serious about laying blame on government, they should blame the local one. Responsibility to perform legally and practically fell first on the mayor of New Orleans . We are now all familiar with Mayor Ray Nagin the black who likes to yell at President Bush for failing to do Nagin' s job. The facts, unfortunately, do not support Nagin' s wailing. As the Washington Times puts it, recent reports show [Nagin] failed to follow through on his own city's emergency-response plan, which acknowledged that thousands of the city's poorest residents would have no way to evacuate the city.'

One wonders how there was' no way' for these people to evacuate the city. We have photographic evidence telling us otherwise. You've probably seen it by now the photo showing 2,000 parked school buses, unused and underwater. How much planning does it require to put people on a bus and leave town, Mayor Nagin?

Instead of doing the obvious, Mayor Nagin (with no positive contribution from Gov. Kathleen Blanco, the other major leader vested with responsibility to address the hurricane disaster) loaded remaining new Orleans residents into the Superdome and the city's convention center. We know how that plan turned out.

About five years ago, in a debate before the National Association of Black Journalists, I stated that if whites were to just leave the United States and let blacks run the country, they would turn America into a ghetto within 10 years. The audience, shall we say, disagreed with me strongly. Now I have to disagree with me. I gave blacks too much credit. It took a mere three days for blacks to turn the Superdome and the convention center into ghettos, rampant with theft, rape and murder.

President Bush is not to blame for the rampant immorality of blacks. Had New Orleans' black community taken action, most would have been out of harm' s way. But most were too lazy, immoral and trifling to do anything productive for themselves.

All Americans must tell blacks this truth. It was blacks moral poverty not their material poverty that cost them dearly in New Orleans. Farrakhan, Jackson, and other race hustlers are to be repudiated for they will only perpetuate this problem by stirring up hatred and applauding moral corruption. New Orleans, to the extent it is to be rebuilt, should be remade into a dependency-free, morally strong city where corruption is opposed and success is applauded. Blacks are obligated to help themselves and not depend on the government to care for them. We are all obligated to tell them so.

The Rev. Jesse Lee Peterson is founder and president of BOND, the Brotherhood Organization of A New Destiny, and author of ' Scam: How the Black Leadership Exploits Black America. '

The Hole we're in - we dug ourselves

I'm sure you heard the story of the person that had a problem with his computer and had called the customer service department where he bought it.

The story goes on and on and finally it gets down to the nitty-gritty. The customer says that it just doesn't work and all the questions the service representative could ask didn't help. Finally the rep. asked when the problem first occurred and the customer said that it happened right after the power went off.

The rep. then asked if he had the original cartons that the computer came in and he said that he did. The rep. then told him to pack it back up and send it to him right away.

The customer was puzzled and asked why? Was it that serious a problem? The rep. then said no - but you're too stupid to own one.

Another story just surfaced about a person who became irate about the killing of animals for our meat. She said, "why don't you get your meat at the store where they make it instead of killing them?"

Yes, ladies and gentlemen, they are out there and they vote. How do you think a black man with only 143 days experience as a Senator and no other could possibly be elected President? You really have to call him the "Shadow". He has the ability to cloud men's minds and make his shortcomings unseen to the voting public. You have to be old enough to know who and what the "Shadow" was to understand this, but he is making a comeback, especially in commercials.

We are really getting a good look at BO and how he handles problems. First, the 2010 elections didn't go his way and the Democrats were soundly rebuked for their actions. Now, all of a sudden, BO is a compromising leader and gets together with the Republicans for passing the tax savings extension.

This wasn't an act out of compassion for the tax paying public, but rather a pure political move to show the voters that he is sympathetic to their wishes.

This man has no principals to guide him but only which side of the bread is the butter on. This is also the man whose minions say that Sarah Palin doesn't have the experience to be President. They also bring out so called polls that show BO ahead by 20 points. That says two things about him. First Sarah hasn't indicated she will run and second it shows that he has so much experience now that he will beat anyone.

BO needs to learn that he is the worst President of all time, including Jimmy Carter. He is a Muslim, liar, killer of allies, socialist, unable to salute the flag, evil, doesn't know how many states in the USA, won't produce his birth certificate or college records, hired corrupt people for his cabinet, does stupid things like using a separate airplane to ferry his dog to them on vacation, takes more vacations than any other president at great expense to the tax payer, had his law license (as well as Michelle's) revoked for dubious reasons. The list could go on and on. This man does NOT represent the best interests of the country or it's people. He is clearly one of the leading candidates that can be classified as having the mark of "666" on his forehead.

Back to Basics

This is from the Wall Street Journal, 11/11/10. Best description of our Prez. I have ever seen. The WSJ is about as reputable a newspaper as there is.

Wall Street Journal Sizes up Obama - They've Got Him Figured Out

"I have this theory about Barack Obama. I think he's led a kind of make-believe life in which money was provided and doors were opened because at some point early on somebody or some group (George Soros anybody?) took a look at this tall, good looking, half-white, half-black, young man with an exotic African/Muslim name and concluded he could be guided toward a life in politics where his facile speaking skills could even put him in the White House.

In a very real way, he has been a young man in a very big hurry Who else do you know has written two memoirs before the age of 45? "Dreams of My Father" was published in 1995 when he was only 34 years old. The "Audacity of Hope" followed in 2006. If, indeed, he did write them himself. There are some who think that his mentor and friend, Bill Ayers, a man who calls himself a "communist with a small 'c'" was the real author.

His political skills consisted of rarely voting on anything that might be deemed controversial. He went from a legislator in the Illinois legislature to the

Senator from that state because he had the good fortune of having Mayor Daley's formidable political machine at his disposal.

He was in the U.S. Senate so briefly that his bid for the presidency was either an act of astonishing self-confidence or part of some greater game plan that had been determined before he first stepped foot in the Capital. How, many must wonder, was he selected to be a 2004 keynote speaker at the Democrat convention that nominated John Kerry when virtually no one had ever even heard of him before?

He outmaneuvered Hillary Clinton in primaries. He took Iowa by storm. A charming young man, an anomaly in the state with a very small black population, he oozed "cool" in a place where agriculture was the antithesis of cool. He dazzled the locals. And he had an army of volunteers drawn to a charisma that hid any real substance.

And then he had the great good fortune of having the Republicans select one of the most inept candidates for the presidency since Bob Dole. And then John McCain did something crazy. He picked Sarah Palin, an unknown female governor from the very distant state of Alaska . It was a ticket that was reminiscent of 1984's Walter Mondale and Geraldine Ferraro and they went down to defeat.

The mainstream political media fell in love with him. It was a schoolgirl crush with febrile commentators like Chris Mathews swooning then and now over the man. The venom directed against McCain and, in particular, Palin, was extraordinary.

Now, nearly a full 2 years into his first term, all of those gilded years leading up to the White House have left him unprepared to be President. Left to his own instincts, he has a talent for saying the wrong thing at the wrong time. It swiftly became a joke that he could not deliver even the briefest of statements without the ever-present Tele-Prompters.

Far worse, however, is his capacity to want to "wish away" some terrible realities, not the least of which is the Islamist intention to destroy America and enslave the West. Any student of history knows how swiftly Islam initially spread. It knocked on the doors of Europe, having gained a foothold in Spain .

The great crowds that greeted him at home or on his campaign "world tour" were no substitute for having even the slightest grasp of history and the reality of a world filled with really bad people with really bad intentions.

Oddly and perhaps even inevitably, his political experience, a cakewalk, has positioned him to destroy the Democrat Party's hold on power in Congress because in the end it was never about the party. It was always about his communist ideology, learned at an early age from family, mentors, college professors, and extreme leftist friends and colleagues.

Obama is a man who could deliver a snap judgment about a Boston police officer who arrested an "obstreperous" Harvard professor-friend, but would warn Americans against "jumping to conclusions" about a mass murderer at Fort Hood who shouted "Allahu Akbar." The absurdity of that was lost on no one. He has since compounded this by calling the Christmas bomber "an isolated extremist" only to have to admit a day or two later that he was part of an al Qaeda plot.

He is a man who could strive to close down our detention facility at Guantanamo even though those released were known to have returned to the battlefield against America . He could even instruct his Attorney General to afford the perpetrator of 9/11 a civil trial when no one else would ever even consider such an obscenity. And he is a man who could wait three days before having anything to say about the perpetrator of yet another terrorist attack on Americans and then have to elaborate on his remarks the following day because his first statement was so lame.

The pattern repeats itself. He either blames any problem on the Bush administration or he naively seeks to wish away the truth.

Knock, knock. Anyone home? Anyone there? Barack Obama exists only as the sock puppet of his handlers, of the people who have maneuvered and manufactured this pathetic individual's life.

When anyone else would quickly and easily produce a birth certificate, this man has spent over a million dollars to deny access to his. Most other documents, the paper trail we all leave in our wake, have been sequestered from review. He has lived a make-believe life whose true facts remain hidden.

We laugh at the ventriloquist's dummy, but what do you do when the dummy is President of the United States of America.

Another paper has jumped in with severe comments about BO. Hopefully, more will wake up and write about the atrocities being perpetrated on the American people.

FINALLY -- SOMEONE IN THE MEDIA HAS STATED THE OBVIOUS. Please share widely!!! Perhaps other writers will grow SPINES. A strong article and hopefully, not the last public newspaper to do so...

http://www.washingtontimes.com/news/2010/jul/22/the-case-for-impeachment-142967590/

KUHNER: President's socialist takeover must be stopped
By Jeffrey T. Kuhner - The Washington Times

President Obama has engaged in numerous high crimes and misdemeanors. The Democratic majority in Congress is in peril as Americans reject his agenda. Yet more must be done: Mr. Obama should be impeached.

He is slowly - piece by painful piece - erecting a socialist dictatorship. We are not there - yet. But he is putting America on that dangerous path. He is undermining our constitutional system of checks and balances; subverting democratic procedures and the rule of law; presiding over a corrupt, gangster regime; and assaulting the very pillars of traditional capitalism. Like Venezuela's leftist strongman, Hugo Chavez, Mr. Obama is bent on imposing a revolution from above - one that is polarizing America along racial, political and ideological lines. Mr. Obama is the most divisive president since Richard Nixon. His policies are Balkanizing the country. It's time for him to go.

He has abused his office and violated his oath to uphold the Constitution. His health care overhaul was rammed through Congress. It was - and remains - opposed by a majority of the people. It could only be passed through bribery and political intimidation. The Louisiana Purchase, the Cornhusker Kickback, the $5 billion Medicaid set-aside for Florida Sen. Bill Nelson -

taxpayer money was used as a virtual slush fund to buy swing votes. Moreover, the law is blatantly unconstitutional: The federal government does not have the right to coerce every citizen to purchase a good or service. This is not in the Constitution, and it represents an unprecedented expansion of power.

Yet Obamacare's most pernicious aspect is its federal funding of abortion. Pro-lifers are now compelled to have their tax dollars used to subsidize insurance plans that allow for the murder of unborn children. This is more than state-sanctioned infanticide. It violates the conscience rights of religious citizens. Traditionalists - evangelicals, Catholics, Baptists, Muslims, Orthodox Jews - have been made complicit in an abomination that goes against their deepest religious values. As the law is implemented (as in Pennsylvania) the consequences of the abortion provisions will become increasingly apparent. The result will be a cultural civil war Pro-lifers will become deeply alienated from society; among many, a secession of the heart is taking place.

Mr. Obama is waging a frontal assault on property rights. The BP oil spill is a case in point. BP clearly is responsible for the spill and its massive economic and environmental damage to the Gulf. There is a legal process for claims to be adjudicated, but Mr. Obama has behaved more like Mr. Chavez or Russia's Vladimir Putin: He has bullied BP into setting up a $20 billion compensation fund administered by an Obama appointee. In other words, the assets of a private company are to be raided to serve a political agenda. Billions will be dispensed arbitrarily in compensation to oil-spill victims - much of it to Democratic constituents. This is cronyism and creeping authoritarianism.

Mr. Obama's multicultural socialism seeks to eradicate traditional America. He has created a command-and-control health care system. He has essentially nationalized the big banks, the financial sector, the automakers and the student loan industry. He next wants to pass "cap-and-trade," which would bring industry and manufacturing under the heel of big government. The state is intervening in every aspect of American life - beyond its constitutionally delegated bounds. Under Mr. Obama, the Constitution has become a meaningless scrap of paper.

To provide the shock troops for his socialist takeover, Mr. Obama calls for "comprehensive immigration reform" - granting amnesty to 12 million to 20 million illegal aliens. This would forge a permanent Democratic electoral majority. It would sound the death knell for our national sovereignty. Amnesty rewards lawlessness and criminal behavior; it signifies the surrender of our porous southern border to a massive illegal invasion. It means the death of American nationhood. We will no longer be a country, but the colony of a global socialist empire.

Rather than defending our homeland, Mr. Obama's Justice Department has sued Arizona for its immigration law. He is siding with criminals against his fellow Americans. His actions desecrate his constitutional oath to protect U.S. citizens from enemies foreign and domestic. He is thus encouraging more illegal immigration as Washington refuses to protect our borders. Mr. Obama's decision on this case is treasonous.

As president, he is supposed to respect the rule of law. Instead, his administration has dropped charges of voter intimidation against members of the New Black Panther Party. This was done even though their menacing behavior was caught on tape: men in military garb brandishing clubs and threatening whites at a polling site. A Justice Department lawyer intimately involved in the case, J. Christian Adams, resigned in protest. Mr. Adams says that under Mr. Obama, there is a new policy: Cases involving black defendants and white victims - no matter how much they cry for justice - are not to be prosecuted. This is more than institutionalized racism. It is an abrogation of civil rights laws. The Justice Department's behavior is illegal. It poses a direct threat to the integrity of our democracy and the sanctity of our electoral process.

Corruption in the administration is rampant. Washington no longer has a government; rather, it has a gangster regime. The Chicago way has become the Washington way. Chief of Staff Rahm Emanuel is a political hit man. He is an amoral, ruthless operator. It was Mr. Emanuel who reached out to Rep. Joe Sestak, Pennsylvania Democrat, offering a high-ranking job in the hopes of persuading Mr. Sestak to pull out of the primary against Sen. Arlen Specter. It was Mr. Emanuel who offered another government position to Andrew Romanoff to do the same in the Colorado Democratic Senate primary. And it was Mr. Emanuel - as the trial of former Illinois Gov. Rod Blagojevich has revealed - who acted as the go-between to try to have Valerie Jarrett parachuted into Mr. Obama's former Senate seat. The only question was: What did Mr. Blagojevich want in exchange?

This is not simply sleazy Chicago machine politics. It is the systematic breaking of the law - bribery, attempt to interfere (and manipulate) elections using taxpayer-funded jobs, influence peddling and abuse of power.

The common misperception on the right is that Mr. Obama is another Jimmy Carter: an incompetent liberal whose presidency is being reduced to rubble under the onslaught of repeated failures. The very opposite, however, is true. He is the most consequential president in our lifetime, transforming America into something our Founding Fathers would find not only unrecognizable, but repugnant. Like all radical revolutionaries, he is consumed by the pursuit of power - attaining it, wielding it and maximizing it. Mr. Obama's fledgling thug state must be stopped.

If Republicans win back Congress in November, they should - and likely will - launch formal investigations into this criminal, scandal-ridden administration. Rep. Darrell Issa, California Republican and ranking member of the Oversight and Government Reform Committee, has promised as much. Mr. Obama has betrayed the American people. Impeachment is the only answer. This usurper must fall.

Jeffrey T. Kuhner is a columnist at The Washington Times and president of the Edmund Burke Institute, a Washington think tank. He is the host of "The Kuhner Show" on WTNT 570-AM (www.talk570.com) from 5 to 7 p.m.

SOURCE: KUHNER: President's socialist takeover must be stopped - Washington Times

Still another paper brings out some of BO's works as being something pushed on the American people, who didn't want it in the first place. Just another attempt to have government control more and more or our freedoms.

Back to Basics

Examiner Editorial:

Obamacare is even worse than critics thought.

Examiner Editorial

September 22, 2010
Much more has been revealed about Obamacare since President Obama, Harry Reid and Nancy Pelosi pushed the bill on Americans six months ago. (J. Scott Applewhite/AP file)

Six months ago, President Obama, Senate Majority Leader Harry Reid and House Speaker Nancy Pelosi rammed Obamacare down the throats of an unwilling American public. Half a year removed from the unprecedented legislative chicanery and backroom dealing that characterized the bill's passage, we know much more about the bill than we did then. A few of the revelations:

Obamacare won't decrease health care costs for the government. According to Medicare's actuary, it will increase costs. The same is likely to happen for privately funded health care.

As written, Obamacare covers elective abortions, contrary to Obama's promise that it wouldn't. This means that tax dollars will be used to pay for a procedure millions of Americans across the political spectrum view as immoral. Supposedly, the Department of Health and Human Services will bar abortion coverage with new regulations but these will likely be tied up for years in litigation, and in the end may not survive the court challenge.

Obamacare won't allow employees or most small businesses to keep the coverage they have and like. By Obama's estimates, as many as 69 percent of employees, 80 percent of small businesses, and 64 percent of large businesses will be forced to change coverage, probably to more expensive plans.

Obamacare will increase insurance premiums -- in some places, it already has. Insurers, suddenly forced to cover clients' children until age 26, have little choice but to raise premiums, and they attribute to Obamacare's mandates a 1 to 9 percent increase. Obama's only method of preventing massive rate increases so far has been to threaten insurers.

Obamacare will force seasonal employers -- especially the ski and amusement park industries -- to pay huge fines, cut hours, or lay off employees.

Obamacare forces states to guarantee not only payment but also treatment for indigent Medicaid patients. With many doctors now refusing to take Medicaid (because they lose money doing so), cash-strapped states could be sued and ordered to increase reimbursement rates beyond their means.

Obamacare imposes a huge non medical tax compliance burden on small business. It will require them to mail IRS 1099 tax forms to every vendor from whom they make purchases of more than $600 in a year, with duplicate forms going to the Internal Revenue Service. Like so much else in the 2,500-page bill, our senators and representatives were apparently unaware of this when they passed the measure.

Obamacare allows the IRS to confiscate part or all of your tax refund if you do not purchase a qualified insurance plan. The bill funds 16,000 new IRS agents to make sure Americans stay in line.

If you wonder why so many American voters are angry, and no longer give Obama the benefit of the doubt on a variety of issues, you need look no further than Obamacare, whose birthday gift to America might just be a GOP congressional majority.

Read more at the Washington Examiner: http://www.washingtonexaminer.com/opinion/Obamacare-is-even-worse-than-critics-thought-960772-103571664.html#ixzz10N0aXRGL

More on Obamacare:

A retired Constitutional lawyer has read the entire proposed health care bill. Read his conclusions and pass this on as you wish. This is stunning!

The Truth About the Health Care Bills - Michael Connelly, Ret. Constitutional Attorney

Well, I have done it! I have read the entire text of proposed House Bill 3200: The Affordable Health Care Choices Act of 2009. I studied it with particular emphasis from my area of expertise, constitutional law. I was frankly concerned that parts of the proposed law that were being discussed might be unconstitutional. What I found was far worse than what I had heard or expected.

To begin with, much of what has been said about the law and its implications is in fact true, despite what the Democrats and the media are saying. The law does provide for rationing of health care, particularly where senior citizens and other classes of citizens are involved, free health care for illegal immigrants, free abortion services, and probably forced participation in abortions by members of the medical profession.

The Bill will also eventually force private insurance companies out of business, and put everyone into a government run system. All decisions about personal health care will ultimately be made by federal bureaucrats, and most of them will not be health care professionals. Hospital admissions, payments to physicians, and allocations of necessary medical devices will be strictly controlled by the government.

However, as scary as all of that is, it just scratches the surface. In fact, I have concluded that this legislation really has no intention of providing affordable health care choices. Instead it is a convenient cover for the most massive transfer of power to the Executive Branch of government that has ever occurred, or even been contemplated If this law or a similar one is adopted, major portions of the Constitution of the United States will effectively have been destroyed.

The first thing to go will be the masterfully crafted balance of power between the Executive, Legislative, and Judicial branches of the U.S. Government. The Congress will be transferring to the Obama Administration authority in a number of different areas over the lives of the American people, and the businesses they own.

The irony is that the Congress doesn't have any authority to legislate in most of those areas to begin with! I defy anyone to read the text of the U.S. Constitution and find any authority granted to the members of Congress to regulate health care.

This legislation also provides for access, by the

appointees of the Obama administration, of all of your personal healthcare direct violation of the specific provisions of the 4th Amendment to the Constitution information, your personal financial information, and the information of your employer, physician, and hospital.   All of this is a protecting against unreasonable searches and seizures.   You can also forget about the right to privacy. That will have been legislated into oblivion regardless of what the 3rd and 4th Amendments may provide.

If you decide not to have healthcare insurance, or if you have private insurance that is not deemed acceptable to the Health Choices Administrator appointed by Obama, there will be a tax imposed on you. It is called a tax instead of a fine because of the intent to avoid application of the due process clause of the 5th Amendment. However , that doesn't work because since there is nothing in the law that allows you to contest or appeal the imposition of the tax, it is definitely depriving someone of property without the due process of law.

So, there are three of those pesky amendments that the far left hate so much, out the original ten in the Bill of Rights, that are effectively nullified by this law   It doesn't stop there though.

The 9th Amendment that provides: The enumeration in the Constitution, of certain rights, shall not be construed to deny or disparage others retained by the people;

The 10th Amendment states: The powers not delegated to the United States by the Constitution, nor prohibited by it to the States, are preserved to the States respectively, or to the people. Under the provisions of this piece of Congressional handiwork neither the people nor the states are going to have any rights or powers at all in many areas that once were theirs to control.

I could write many more pages about this legislation, but I think you get the idea. This is not about health care; it is about seizing power and limiting rights. Article 6 of the Constitution requires the members of both houses of Congress to "be bound by oath or affirmation to support the Constitution." If I was a member of Congress I would not be able to vote for this legislation or anything like it, without feeling I was violating that sacred oath or affirmation. If I voted for it anyway, I would hope the American people would hold me accountable.

For those who might doubt the nature of this threat, I suggest they consult the source, the US Constitution, and Bill of Rights. There you can see exactly what we are about to have taken from us.

Michael Connelly, Retired attorney,
Constitutional Law Instructor
Carrollton , Texas

This following may sound like a parody on the President, but it is really happening:

How's this for apocalyptic literature. This was written by a pastor's wife in biblical prose as a commentary of current events. It is brilliant.

And it came to pass in the Age of Insanity that the people of the land called America, having lost their morals, their initiative, and their will to defend their liberties, chose as their Supreme Leader that person known as "The One."

He emerged from the vapors with a message that had no meaning; but He hypnotized the people telling them, "I am sent to save you." My lack of experience, my questionable ethics, my monstrous ego, and my association with evil doers are of no consequence. I shall save you with hope and Change. Go, therefore, and proclaim throughout the land that he who proceeded me is evil, that he has defiled the nation, and that all he has built must be destroyed.. And the people rejoiced, for even though they knew not what "The One" would do, he had promised that it was good; and they believed. And "The One" said " We live in the greatest country in the world. Help me change everything about it!" And the people said, "Hallelujah! Change is good!"

Then He said, "We are going to tax the rich fat-cats." And the people said "Sock it to them!" "And redistribute their wealth.." And the people said, "Show us the money!" And the he said, "redistribution of wealth is good for everybody."

And Joe the plumber asked, "Are you kidding me? You're going to steal my money and give it to the deadbeats??" And "The One" ridiculed and taunted him, and Joe's personal records were hacked and publicized. One lone reporter asked, "Isn't that Marxist policy?" And she was banished from the kingdom!

Then a citizen asked, "With no foreign relations experience and having zero military experience or knowledge, how will you deal with radical terrorists?" And "The One" said, "Simple. I shall sit with them and talk with them and show them how nice we really are; and they will forget that they ever wanted to kill us all!" And the people said, "Hallelujah!! We are safe at last, and we can beat our weapons into free cars for the people!"

Then "The One" said "I shall give 95% of you lower taxes." And one, lone voice said, "But 40% of us don't pay ANY taxes." So "The One" said, "Then I shall give you some of the taxes the fat-cats pay!" And the people said, "Hallelujah! Show us the money!" Then "The One" said, "I shall tax your Capital Gains when you sell your homes!" And the people yawned and the slumping housing market collapsed. And He said. "I shall mandate employer-funded health care for every worker and raise the minimum wage.. And I shall give every person unlimited healthcare and medicine and transportation to the clinics." And the people said, "Give me some of that!" Then he said, "I shall penalize employers who ship jobs overseas." And the people said, "Where's my rebate check?"

Then "The One" said, "I shall bankrupt the coal industry and electricity rates will skyrocket!" And the people said, "Coal is dirty, coal is evil, no more coal! But we don't care for that part about higher electric rates." So "The One" said, Not to worry. If your rebate isn't enough to cover your expenses, we shall bail you out. Just sign up with the ACORN and you troubles are over!"

Then He said, "Illegal immigrants feel scorned and slighted.. Let's grant them amnesty, Social Security, free education, free lunches, free medical care, bi-lingual signs and guaranteed housing...." And the people said, "Hallelujah!" and they made him king!

And so it came to pass that employers, facing spiraling costs and ever-higher taxes, raised their prices and laid off workers. Others simply gave up and went out of business and the economy sank like unto a rock dropped from a cliff. The bank banking industry was destroyed. Manufacturing slowed to a crawl. And more of the people were without a means of support..

Then "The One" said, "I am the "the One"- The Messiah - and I'm here to save you! We shall just print more money so everyone will have enough!" But our foreign trading partners said unto Him. "Wait a minute. Your dollar is not worth a pile of camel dung! You will have to pay more... And "The One" said, "Wait a minute. That is unfair!!" And the world said, "Neither are these other idiotic programs you have embraced. Lo, you have become a Socialist state and a second-rate power. Now you shall play by our rules!"

And the people cried out, "Alas, alas!! What have we done?" But yea verily, it was too late. The people set upon The One and spat upon him and stoned him, and his name was dung.. And the once mighty nation was no more; and the once proud people were without sustenance or shelter or hope. And the Change "The One" had given them was as like unto a poison that had destroyed them and like a whirlwind that consumed all that they had built.

And the people beat their chests in despair and cried out in anguish, "give us back our nation and our pride and our hope!!" But it was too late, and their homeland was no more.

You may think this a fairy tale, but it's not. It's happening RIGHT NOW
A sad scenario indeed.   However, it doesn't take a rocket scientist to see that these things are happening

right now. Those that have the most to gain in keeping our country on the right track are the ones that are destroying it because they have hooked up, lock, stock and barrel, with "The One". Even if they are having doubts, they still hang on so their dream of getting something for nothing won't be broken.

It's enough to make you sick. How do you show these people the error of their ways? Surely they would straighten up if they knew the truth. Don't count on it.

Let's compare again the Presidencies of G. W. Bush and BO:

If George W. Bush had doubled the national debt, which had taken more than two centuries to accumulate, in one year, would you have approved?

If George W. Bush had then proposed to double the debt again within 10 years, would you have approved?

If George W. Bush had criticized a state law that he admitted he never even read, would you think that he is just an ignorant hot head?

If George W. Bush joined the country of Mexico and sued a state in the United States to force that state to continue to allow illegal immigration, would you question his patriotism and wonder who's side he was on?

If George W. Bush had put 87000 workers out of work by arbitrarily placing a moratorium on offshore oil drilling on companies that have one of the best safety records of any industry because one company had an accident would you have agreed?

If George W. Bush had used a forged document as the basis of the moratorium that would render 87000 American workers unemployed would you support him?

If George W. Bush had been the first President to need a TelePrompTer installed to be able to get through a press conference, would you have laughed and said this is more proof of how inept he is on his own and is really controlled by men behind the scenes?

If George W. Bush had spent hundreds of thousands of taxpayer dollars to take Laura Bush to a play in NYC, would you have approved?

If George W. Bush had reduced your retirement plan's holdings of GM stock by 90% and given the unions a majority stake in GM, would you have approved?

If George W. Bush had made a joke at the expense of the Special Olympics, would you have approved?

If George W. Bush had given Gordon Brown a set of inexpensive and incorrectly formatted DVDs, when Gordon Brown had given him a thoughtful and historically significant gift, would you have approved?

If George W. Bush had given the Queen of England an iPod containing videos of his speeches, would you have thought this embarrassingly narcissistic and tacky?

If George W. Bush had bowed to the King of Saudi Arabia , would you have approved?

If George W. Bush had visited Austria and made reference to the nonexistent "Austrian language," would you have brushed it off as a minor slip?

If George W. Bush had filled his cabinet and circle of advisers with people who cannot seem to keep current in their income taxes, would you have approved?

If George W. Bush had stated that there were 57 states in the United States, would you have said that he is clueless or even fit to be President?

If George W. Bush would have flown all the way to Denmark to make a five minute speech about how the Olympics would benefit him walking out his front door in Texas , would you have thought he was a self important, conceited, egotistical jerk?

If George W. Bush had been so Spanish illiterate as to refer to "Cinco de Cuatro" in front of the Mexican ambassador when it was the 5th of May (Cinco de Mayo), and continued to flub it when he tried again, would you have winced in embarrassment?

If George W. Bush had misspelled the word "advice" would you have hammered him for it for years like Dan Quayle and potatoes as proof of what a dunce he is?

If George W. Bush had burned 9,000 gallons of jet fuel to go plant a single tree on Earth Day, would you have concluded he's a hypocrite?

If George W. Bush's administration had okayed Air Force One flying low over millions of people followed by a jet fighter in downtown Manhattan causing widespread panic, would you have wondered whether they actually get what happened on 9-11?

If George W. Bush had failed to send relief aid to flood victims throughout the Midwest with more people killed or made homeless than in New Orleans, would you want it made into a major ongoing political issue with claims of racism and incompetence?

If George W. Bush had created the position of 32 Czars who report directly to him, bypassing the House and Senate on much of what is happening in America , would you have approved?

If George W. Bush had ordered the firing of the CEO of a major corporation, even though he had no constitutional authority to do so, would you have approved?

So, tell me again, what is it about Obama that makes him so brilliant and impressive? Can't think of anything? Don't worry. He's done all this in 15 months -- so you'll have two years and nine months to come up with an answer.

Every statement is factual and directly attributable to Barrack Hussein Obama. Every bumble is a matter of record and completely verifiable.

Who's Responsible?

The article below is completely neutral, not anti republican or democrat.

Charlie Reese, a retired reporter for the Orlando Sentinel has hit the nail directly on the head, defining clearly who it is that in the final analysis must assume responsibility for the judgments made that impact each one of us every day.

It's a short but good read. Worth the time. Worth remembering!

545 vs. 300,000,000

EVERY CITIZEN NEEDS TO READ THIS AND THINK ABOUT WHAT THIS JOURNALIST HAS SCRIPTED IN THIS MESSAGE. READ IT AND THEN REALLY THINK ABOUT OUR CURRENT POLITICAL DEBACLE.

Charley Reese has been a journalist for 49 years.

545 PEOPLE -- By Charlie Reese

Politicians are the only people in the world who create problems and then campaign against them.

Have you ever wondered, if both the Democrats and the Republicans are against deficits, WHY do we have deficits?

Have you ever wondered, if all the politicians are against inflation and high taxes, WHY do we have inflation and high taxes?

You and I don't propose a federal budget. The president does.

You and I don't have the Constitutional authority to vote on appropriations. The House of Representatives does.

You and I don't write the tax code, Congress does.

You and I don't set fiscal policy, Congress does.

You and I don't control monetary policy, the Federal Reserve Bank does.

One hundred senators, 435 congressmen, one president, and nine Supreme Court justices equates to 545 human beings out of the 300 million are directly, legally, morally, and individually responsible for the domestic problems that plague this country.

I excluded the members of the Federal Reserve Board because that problem was created by the Congress. In 1913, Congress delegated its

Constitutional duty to provide a sound currency to a federally chartered, but private, central bank.

I excluded all the special interests and lobbyists for a sound reason. They have no legal authority. They have no ability to coerce a senator, a congressman, or a president to do one cotton-picking thing. I don't care if they offer a politician $1 million dollars in cash. The politician has the power to accept or reject it. No matter what the lobbyist promises, it is the legislator's responsibility to determine how he votes.

Those 545 human beings spend much of their energy convincing you that what they did is not their fault. They cooperate in this common con regardless of party.

What separates a politician from a normal human being is an excessive amount of gall. No normal human being would have the gall of a Speaker, who stood up and criticized the President for creating deficits.... . The president can only propose a budget. He cannot force the Congress to accept it.

The Constitution, which is the supreme law of the land, gives sole responsibility to the House of Representatives for originating and approving appropriations and taxes. Who is the speaker of the House? Nancy Pelosi. She is the leader of the majority party. She and fellow House members, not the president, can approve any budget they want. If the president vetoes it, they can pass it over his veto if they agree to.

It seems inconceivable to me that a nation of 300 million can not replace 545 people who stand convicted -- by present facts -- of incompetence and irresponsibility. I can't think of a single domestic problem that is not traceable directly to those 545 people. When you fully grasp the plain truth that 545 people exercise the power of the federal government, then it must follow that what exists is what they want to exist.

If the tax code is unfair, it's because they want it unfair.

If the budget is in the red, it's because they want it in the red .

If the Army & Marines are in IRAQ , it's because they want them in IRAQ

If they do not receive social security but are on an elite retirement plan not available to the people, it's because they want it that way.

There are no insoluble government problems.

Do not let these 545 people shift the blame to bureaucrats, whom they hire and whose jobs they can abolish; to lobbyists, whose gifts and advice they can reject; to regulators, to whom they give the power to regulate and from whom they can take this power. Above all, do not let them con you into the belief that there exists disembodied mystical forces like "the economy," "inflation," or "politics" that prevent them from doing what they take an oath to do.

Those 545 people, and they alone, are responsible.

They, and they alone, have the power..

They, and they alone, should be held accountable by the people who are their bosses. Provided the voters have the gumption to manage their own employees... We should vote all of them out of office and clean up their mess!

Charlie Reese is a former columnist of the Orlando Sentinel Newspaper.

What you do with this article now that you have read it......... Is up to you.
Sales Tax
School Tax
Liquor Tax
Luxury Tax
Excise Taxes
Property Tax
Cigarette Tax
Medicare Tax
Inventory Tax

Real Estate Tax
Well Permit Tax
Fuel Permit Tax
Inheritance Tax
Road Usage Tax
CDL license Tax
Dog License Tax
State Income Tax
Food License Tax
Vehicle Sales Tax
Gross Receipts Tax
Social Security Tax
Service Charge Tax
Fishing License Tax
Federal Income Tax
Building Permit Tax
IRS Interest Charges
Hunting License Tax
Marriage License Tax
Corporate Income Tax
Personal Property Tax
Accounts Receivable Tax
Recreational Vehicle Tax
Workers Compensation Tax
Watercraft Registration Tax
Telephone Usage Charge Tax
Telephone Federal Excise Tax
Telephone State and Local Tax
IRS Penalties (tax on top of tax)
State Unemployment Tax (SUTA)
Federal Unemployment Tax (FUTA)

Telephone Minimum Usage Surcharge Tax
Telephone Federal Universal Service Fee Tax
Gasoline Tax (currently 44.75 cents per gallon)
Utility Taxes Vehicle License Registration Tax
Telephone Federal, State and Local Surcharge Taxes
Telephone Recurring and Nonrecurring Charges Tax

Not one of these taxes existed 100 years ago, & our nation was the most prosperous in the world. We had absolutely no national debt, had the largest middle class in the world, and Mom stayed home to raise the kids.

What in the hell happened? Can you spell 'politicians?

GO AHEAD - - - BE AN AMERICAN!!!

Now BO has appointed some minions called "Czars". These people only answer to BO and no one else:

Stunning.................There are very few of us who know what all the CZAR's do up in D.C............Here is their names and job descriptions.........should be educational to ALL AMERICANS.............no matter what your political agenda..........where did all these people come from and who appointed them?

OBAMA'S "CZARS"—Read who they are and realize what they want to do.

Richard Holbrook, AfghanistanCzar (just died)
Ultra liberal anti gun former Gov. Of New Mexico. Pro Abortion and legal drug use. Dissolve the 2nd Amendment

Ed Montgomery, Auto recovery Czar
Black radical anti business activist. Affirmative Action and Job Preference for blacks. Univ of Maryland Business School Dean teaches US business has caused world poverty. ACORN board member. Communist DuBois Club member.

Jeffrey Crowley, AIDS Czar
Radical Homosexual.. A Gay Rights activist. Believes in Gay Marriage and especially, a Special Status for homosexuals only, including complete free health care for gays.

Alan Bersin, Border Czar
The former failed superintendent of San Diego . Ultra Liberal friend of Hilary Clinton.   Served as Border Czar under Janet Reno - to keep borders open to illegal's without interference from US

David J. Hayes, California Water Czar
Sr. Fellow of radical environmentalist group, "Progress Policy". No training or experience in water management whatsoever.

Ron Bloom, Car Czar

Auto Union worker. Anti business & anti nuclear. Has worked hard to force US auto makers out of business. Sits on the Board of Chrysler which is now Auto Union owned. How did this happen?

Dennis Ross, Central Region Czar

Believes US policy has caused Mid East wars. Obama apologist to the world. Anti gun and completely pro abortion.

Lynn Rosenthal, Domestic Violence Czar

Director of the National Network to End Domestic Violence. Vicious anti male feminist. Supported male castration. Imagine?

Gil Kerlikowske, Drug Czar

devoted lobbyist for every restrictive gun law proposal, Former Chief of Police in Liberal Seattle. Believes no American should own a firearm. Supports legalization of all drugs

Paul Volcker, EconomicCzar

Head of Fed Reserve under Jimmy Carter when US economy nearly failed. Obama appointed head of the Economic Recovery Advisory Board which engineered the Obama economic disaster to US economy. Member of anti business "Progressive Policy" organization

Carol rBower, Energy and Environment Czar
Political Radical Former head of EPA - known for anti-business activism. Strong anti-gun ownership.

Joshua DuBois, Faith Based Czar
Political Black activist-Degree in Black Nationalism. Anti gun ownership lobbyist. WHAT THE HELL DOES A FAITH BASED CZAR DO???????????

Cameron Davis, Great Lakes Czar
Chicago radical anti business environmentalist. Blames George Bush for "Poisoning the water that minorities have to drink." No experience or training in water management. Former ACORN Board member (what does that tell us?)

Van Jones, Green Jobs Czar
(since resigned).. Black activist Member of American communist Party and San Francisco Communist Party who said Geo Bush caused the 911 attack and wanted Bush investigated by the World Court for war crimes. Black activist with strong anti-white views.

Daniel Fried, Guantanamo Closure Czar
Human Rights activist for Foreign Terrorists. Believes America has caused the war on terrorism. Believes terrorists have rights above and beyond Americans.

Nancy-Ann DeParle, Health Czar
Former head of Medicare / Medicaid. Strong Health Care Rationing proponent. She is married to a reporter for The New York Times.

Vivek Kundra, Information Czar
Born in New Delhi, India. Controls all public information, including labels and news releases. Monitors all private Internet emails. (hello?)

Todd Stern, International Climate Czar
Anti business former White House chief of Staff-Strong supporter of the Kyoto Accord. Pushing hard for Cap and Trade. Blames US business for Global warming. Anti- US business prosperity.

Dennis Blair, Intelligence Czar
Ret. Navy. Stopped US guided missile program as "provocative". Chair of ultra liberal "Council on Foreign Relations" which blames American organizations for regional wars.

George Mitchell, Mideast Peace Czar
Fmr. Sen from Maine Left wing radical. Has said Israel should be split up into "2 or 3" smaller more manageable plots". (God forbid) A true Anti-nuclear anti-gun & pro homosexual "special rights" advocate.

Kenneth Feinberg, Pay Czar
Chief of Staff to TED KENNEDY.   Lawyer who got rich off the 911 victims payoffs.   (horribly true)

Cass Sunstein, Regulatory Czar
Liberal activist judge believes free speech needs to be limited for the "common good". Essentially against 1st amendment.   Rules against personal freedoms many times -like private gun ownership and right to free speech. This guy has to be run out of Washington !!

John Holdren, Science Czar
Fierce ideological environmentalist, Sierra Club, Anti business activist.   Claims US business has caused world poverty. No Science training.

Earl Devaney, Stimulus Accountability Czar
Spent career trying to take guns away from American citizens. Believes in Open Borders to Mexico. Author of   statement blaming US gun stores for drug war in Mexico .

J. Scott Gration, Sudan Czar
Native of Democratic Republic of Congo.   Believes US does little to help Third World countries.   Council of foreign relations, asking for higher US taxes to support United Nations.

Herb Allison, TARP Czar

Fannie Mae CEO responsible for the US recession by using real estate mortgages to back up the US stock market. Caused millions of people to lose their life savings.

John Brennan, Terrorism Czar

Anti CIA activist. No training in diplomatic or gov. affairs. Believes Open Borders to Mexico and a dialog with terrorists and has suggested Obama disband US military A TOTAL MORON !!!!!

Aneesh Chopra, Technology Czar

No Technology training. Worked for the Advisory Board Company, a health care think tank for hospitals. Anti doctor activist. Supports Obama Health care Rationing and salaried doctors working exclusively for the Gov. health care plan.

Adolfo Carrion Jr., Urban Affairs Czar

Puerto Rican born Anti American activist and leftist group member in Latin America . Millionaire "slum lord" of the Bronx , NY. Owns many lavish homes and condos which he got from "sweetheart" deals with labor unions. Wants higher taxes on middle class to pay for minority housing and health care.

Ashton Carter, Weapons Czar

Leftist. Wants all private weapons in US destroyed. Supports UN ban on firearms ownership inAmerica .. No Other "policy"

<u>Gary Samore, WMD Policy Czar</u>
Former US Communist.   Wants US to destroy all
WMD unilaterally as a show of good faith.   Has no
other "policy".

How lucky are we that these are the people who are
helping President Obama in the RUNNING of our
country and the White House?

I printed these names before in another book, but it's
good to review them again.   Please look at their
qualifications and tell me that they are suited for work
in the US government.   They should be run out of
town on a rail.   If any other President had appointed
such unqualified people to these high ranking jobs the
newspapers would cry bloody murder.   As it is now -
you don't hear anything about these impostors.   Of
course if anything is said now - we must be racist or
some kind of terrorist. After all - the President of the
United States appointed these jerks - so it must be
OK.

I hope you are starting to get the idea that all is not
well in Washington DC.   We have to turn it around
before it is too late. I, for one, do not want to hear my
kids, grandchildren or great-grandchildren say that my
generation had an opportunity to change things and
we didn't do it.   Much of this garbage will not effect
me, because of my age, but certainly will effect those
that come after me. I will not rest as long as I can see
to write and be able to speak of these "constitution

busters". The TEA Party didn't just happen because someone wanted to start a movement. It started because thousands and thousands of people are fed up and want to take this country back to our "BASICS".

Back to Basics

Who is BO?

Overwhelm The System
Wayne Allyn Root

Barrack Obama is no fool. He is not incompetent. To the contrary, he is brilliant. He knows exactly what he's doing. He is purposely overwhelming the U.S. economy to create systemic failure, economic crisis and social chaos -- thereby destroying capitalism and our country from within.

Barack Obama is my college classmate (Columbia University, class of '83). As Glenn Beck correctly predicted from day one, Obama is following the plan of Cloward and Piven, two professors at Columbia University. They outlined a plan to socialize America by overwhelming the system with government spending and entitlement demands. Add up the clues below. Taken individually they're alarming. Taken as a whole, it is a brilliant, Machiavellian game plan to turn the United States into a socialist/Marxist state with a permanent majority that desperately needs government for survival ... and can be counted on to always vote for bigger government. Why not? They have no responsibility to pay for it.

- Universal health care. The health care bill had very little to do with health care. It had everything to do with unionizing millions of hospital and health care workers, as well as adding 15,000 to 20,000 new IRS agents (who will join government employee unions). Obama doesn't care that giving free health care to 30 million Americans will add trillions to the national debt. What he does care about is that it cements the dependence of those 30 million voters to Democrats and big government. Who but a socialist revolutionary would pass this reckless spending bill in the middle of a depression?

- Cap and trade. Like health care legislation having nothing to do with health care, cap and trade has nothing to do with global warming. It has everything to do with redistribution of income, government control of the economy and a criminal payoff to Obama's biggest contributors. Those powerful and wealthy unions and contributors (like GE, which owns NBC, MSNBC and CNBC) can then be counted on to support everything Obama wants. They will kickback hundreds of millions of dollars in contributions to Obama and the Democratic Party to keep them in power. The bonus is that all the new taxes on Americans with bigger cars, bigger homes and businesses helps Obama "spread the wealth around."

- Make Puerto Rico a state. Why? Who's asking for a 51st state? Who's asking for millions of new welfare recipients and government entitlement addicts in the middle of a depression?   Certainly not American taxpayers. But this has been Obama's plan all along. His goal is to add two new Democrat senators, five

Democrat congressman and a million loyal Democratic voters who are dependent on big government.

- Legalize 12 million illegal immigrants. Just giving these 12 million potential new citizens free health care alone could overwhelm the system and bankrupt America. But it adds 12 million reliable new Democrat voters who can be counted on to support big government. Add another few trillion dollars in welfare, aid to dependent children, food stamps, free medical, education, tax credits for the poor, and eventually Social Security.

-- Stimulus and bailouts. Where did all that money go? It went to Democrat contributors, organizations (ACORN), and unions -- including billions of dollars to save or create jobs of government employees across the country. It went to save GM and Chrysler so that their employees could keep paying union dues. It went to AIG so that Goldman Sachs could be bailed out (after giving Obama almost $1 million in contributions). A staggering $125 billion went to teachers (thereby protecting their union dues). All those public employees will vote loyally Democrat to protect their bloated salaries and pensions that are bankrupting America . The country goes broke, future generations face a bleak future, but Obama, the Democrat Party, government, and the unions grow more powerful. The ends justify the means.

-- Raise taxes on small business owners, high-income earners, and job creators. Put the entire burden on only the top 20 percent of taxpayers, redistribute the income, punish success, and reward those who did nothing to deserve it (except vote for Obama). Reagan wanted to dramatically cut taxes in order to starve the government. Obama wants to dramatically raise taxes to starve his political opposition.

With the acts outlined above, Obama and his regime have created a vast and rapidly expanding constituency of voters dependent on big government; a vast privileged class of public employees who work for big government; and a government dedicated to destroying capitalism and installing themselves as socialist rulers by overwhelming the system.

Add it up and you've got the perfect Marxist scheme -- all devised by my Columbia University college classmate Barack Obama using the Cloward and Piven Plan.

P.S. It will work unless "We the people" stop him, and do so very soon.There are people who will simply read and delete this.   There are others that are so wrapped up with Obama-mania that they will never accept any criticism of him. There are those that say, 'I'm too old to worry about this ... it's not going to affect me'!   Finally, there are professional blood-suckers that live off everyone else's sweat -- they want more 'Free Stuff'. And we all know where they stand. If you care about your future, or maybe your children or grandchildren's future, do something now. Vote the bums out of office this November. And, make Obama a one-term president.

More from Wayne_Allyn_Root

The great mystery..............

WHO IS HE? Ever wondered why no one ever came forward from Obama's past saying they knew him, attended school with him, was his friend, etc. Not one person has ever come forward from his past.

VERY, VERY STRANGE...

This should really be a cause for great concern. To those who voted for him, you have elected the biggest unqualified fraud that America has ever known. Sort of adds credence to the idea of The Manchurian Candidate thing happening here!

Let's face it. As insignificant as we all are ... someone whom we went to school with remembers our name or face ... Someone remembers we were the clown or the dork or the brain or the quiet one or the bully or something about us.

George Stephanopoulos of ABC News said the same thing during the 2008 campaign. He questioned why no one has acknowledged the president was in their classroom or ate in the same cafeteria or made >impromptu speeches on campus.

Stephanopoulos also was a classmate of Obama at Columbia -- the class of 1984. He says he never had a single class with him.

While he is such a great orator, why doesn't anyone in Obama's college class remember him?   And, why won't he allow Columbia to release his records?

NOBODY REMEMBERS OBAMA AT COLUMBIA !

Looking for evidence of Obama's past, Fox News contacted 400 Columbia University students from the period when Obama claims to have been there, but none remembered him.

Wayne Allyn Root was, like Obama, a political science major at Columbia who also graduated in 1983. In 2008, Root says of Obama, "I don't know a single person at Columbia that knew him, and they all know me. I don't have a classmate who ever knew Barack Obama at Columbia, EVER!

Nobody recalls him. Root adds that he was also, like Obama, "Class of '83 political science, pre-law" and says, "You don't get more exact or closer than that." Never met him in my life, don't know anyone who ever met him. At the class reunion, our 20th reunion five years ago, who was asked to be the speaker of the class? Me. No one ever heard of Barack! And five years ago, nobody even knew who he was.

The guy who writes the class notes, who's kind of the, as we say in New York, the macha who knows everybody, has yet to find a person, a human who ever met him."

Obama's photograph does not appear in the school's yearbook and Obama consistently declines requests to talk about his years at Columbia, provide school records, or provide the name of any former classmates or friends while at Columbia.

http://en.wikipedia.org/wiki/Wayne_Allyn_Root#column-one
http://en.wikipedia.org/wiki/Wayne_Allyn_Root#column-one%3E;

NOTE: Root graduated as Valedictorian from his high school, Thornton-Donovan School, then graduated from Columbia University in 1983 as a Political Science major in the same class that Barack Hussein Obama was supposed to have been in.

Some other interesting questions..

Why was Obama's law license inactivated in 2002?

Why was Michelle's law license inactivated by Court Order?

It is circulating that according to the U.S. Census, there is only one Barack Obama but 27 Social Security numbers and over 80 aliases.

The Social Security number he uses now originated in Connecticut where he is never reported to have lived.

No wonder all his records are sealed!

You have to wonder if the mainstream press can find out all about President Nixon and who "Deep Throat" was and all about President Bush's Air National Guard records that they would relish digging into BO's past. Maybe it's because they don't want to.

The stonewalling is similar to when President Roosevelt was in office. The press knew, but very few others knew that he was paralyzed from the waist down. That didn't have anything to do with his ability to be President, but it shows how these things can happen and the public is unaware. The press only does reporting that the owners believe is newsworthy.

The Day of Reckoning is Here!

Please believe me when I say that I hope I'm wrong. However, the handwriting is on the wall and the chickens are coming home to roost.

Approximately 46 out of the 50 states could file bankruptcy in the next 6 - 12 months. Ten of those states are in imminent danger of bankruptcy. Among them are California, Arizona, Rhode Island, Michigan, Oregon, New Jersey, Florida, Nevada, Illinois and Wisconsin.

These states will run out of "bailout money" early in 2011 and the federal government doesn't have any more available. I'm sure the "stop spending mentality" will have kicked in by then.

Approximately 10% of the cities in the US will also be in, or close to, bankruptcy. Can you imagine what this will mean to us, normal citizens? Our beloved "green back" will be devalued severely and will fall off the elevated pedestal of being the world's reserve currency. That means that the dollar will not be the preferred currency that the world trades with.

One of the reasons that California is in so much trouble is documented in the following article:

California - Dumb, Dumber & Dumbest

If California was a movie, it would have to be called Dumb, Dumber and Dumbest. In contrast to the trend around the country in which Republicans were elected resoundingly rejecting Obama and all his Socialist Schemes, California continues down the Socialist path toward complete bankruptcy. 72 year old, Socialist Jerry Brown, the former Governor of California, 28 years ago, referred to then as Governor Moon Beam, was reelected to serve as the Governor of California defeating Republican Meg Whitman, the former CEO of E-Bay.

Brown is owned lock, stock and barrel by the public employee unions that are bankrupting the state. There is currently about $100 billion of unfunded public employee union pension liability that will hit the state of California. Brown actually caused the mess years ago by signing the bill that allowed for collective bargaining by public employee unions.

And, the Socialist controlled legislature, with the signature of current RINO Governor Arnold Schwarzenegger, just approved a budget to close a $20 billion deficit that was all smoke and mirrors, including higher revenue assumptions than will occur and an assumption that President Obama is going to give California $5 Billion in the next fiscal year. Since all appropriations begin in the House of Representatives, that is now controlled by Republicans, that $5 billion is a pipe dream.

So Governor Brown, who will not be able to cross the public employee unions, is walking into a real mess. The unions are advocating tax increases, which Brown committed during the campaign, will not happen without a vote of the people. We will see how long that promise is kept!! There are currently more than 200,000 employees on the state payroll and that does not include local public employees like teachers, cops and firemen. 50,000 of them would have to be laid off, to deal with California's annual deficit, which is almost impossible and will not happen under Jerry Brown. Remember, whose bread you eat, whose song you sing. Brown has been feeding at the union trough for years so he just can't break the habit.

California already has among the highest taxes in the nation and all sorts of job killer laws that have been driving companies and jobs out of California for years. Current official unemployment is above 12%; but the real number is probably 16%, if all are counted. Raising taxes and adding even more regulations, likely under Brown, will insure perpetual unemployment in California. No company in their right mind would expand, or open up a new business in California.

Ultimately, California will have to file bankruptcy, which will include a default on California bonds, that now have junk bond status, to deal with its deficit spending. The only problem is that the Socialist State Legislature enacted legislation, signed by one of the

Socialist Governors years ago, that says in the event of bankruptcy, the state cannot abrogate its public employee union contracts and pension liability. I doubt this will stand up in a bankruptcy court; but this law is on the books.

And to add a nail to the coffin, the voters of California voted to implement Assembly Bill 32, the California version of CAP & TAX that will raise the cost of energy for all along with the cost of all goods and services. Proposition 23, the initiative on the ballot that would have delayed implementation until unemployment was down to 5.5%, failed by a 61.1% to 38.9% vote. The majority of voters, 3 to 1 Socialist in California, are simply crazy and or they have such a poor understanding of Economic 101, that logic and common sense just cannot prevail.

Finally, the majority of voters in California reelected Senator Barbara Boxer, by far the most incompetent Senator in the US Congress. Even her home town newspaper, the San Francisco Chronicle, did not endorse Boxer saying that her 28 year career in Congress was "undistinguished". That is a code word for saying that Boxer is so left wing and polarizing that she has accomplished absolutely nothing in her 28 years in Congress.

So we have Dumb, the election of Jerry Brown as Governor, Dumber, the rejection of Proposition 23, and Dumbest, the reelection of Senator Barbara

Boxer. California is lost and on a death spiral until such time as the people of California wake up and take back their state. In any case, we can see what happens when Socialists control all branches of government. Entitlements explode, taxes go through the roof and jobs are destroyed.

What is happening in California is another reason we must take back our country by electing Conservatives that support free market capitalism, limited government, lower taxes and less regulation, real energy independence and health care reform, a strong national defense, including securing our border and fighting Terrorism, the right to bear arms, the sanctity of life and family values that are the foundation of our nation. This is platform, which is supported by the majority of the American people, is the only way to restore economic growth and job creation in America.

We must also elect Conservatives that adhere to the Constitution, as written by our Founding Fathers, not as contrived by the left wing media, Socialists in the last 97 years, former Presidents, Congresses or the Courts. We can do it. We will do it to preserve our freedom, our nation and way of life and for the sake of our children and grandchildren. We certainly can't let our elected representatives in Washington do to our nation what the Socialists have done to California. Yep, a movie about California would be certainly be called Dumb, Dumber and Dumbest.

A number of states smartened up in the 2010 election and dumped their liberal Governors, Senators and Representatives. California didn't. And I always thought California led the way in so many areas. I guess it really does in being stupid. The same old politicians returned to office along with "has been" Jerry Brown. Can he redeem himself this time around? He didn't just step in the crap, but sunk right up to his eyeballs. Now we'll see if his alligator mouth will overload his hummingbird ass.

California has a growing problem. Businesses just keep leaving the state in growing numbers. Here is a list of just some of them:

Flood Of Calif. Businesses Abandon State
Numerous California businesses are packing up their bags and trading in the blue skies and hot weather to head east.

The Courier obtained a copy of the businesses leaving California this year.
They are:

1. Alza Corp. in 2007 eliminated about 600 jobs in drug R&D while also exiting its Mountain View HQ. At the time the company said that its 1,200-person Vacaville facility will continue to operate. But the Vacaville Reporter on Oct. 23, 2009 revealed that the plant is being offered for sale by J&J, its parent

company. It,s unclear if more layoffs are in the facility's future.

2. American AVK, a producer of fire hydrants and other water-related products, moved from Fresno to Minden, Nevada.

3. American Racing moved its auto-wheel production to Mexico, ending most of its 47-year operation in California.

4. Apple Computer has expanded in other states, most recently with a $1 billion facility planned for North Carolina.

5. Audix Corporation relocated from Redwood City and to accommodate growth moved to a 78,000-square-foot facility in Wilson, Oregon.

6. Apria Healthcare Group of Lake Forest is shifting jobs from California to Overland Park, Kansas, a K.C. suburb.

7. Assurant Inc. cut 325 jobs in Orange County and consolidated positions in Georgia, Ohio and South Carolina.

8. Automobile Club of Southern California placed 1,100 jobs in Texas.

9. Barefoot Motors, a small "green" manufacturer, moved from Sonoma and will grow in Ashland, Oregon.

10. Bazz Houston Co. located in Garden Grove, has slowly been building a workforce of about 35 people in Tijuana. In early 2010 the company said it expects to move more jobs to Mexico, citing cost and regulatory difficulties in Southern California .

11. Beckman Coulter, a biomedical test equipment manufacturer headquartered in Brea, relocated part of its Palo Alto facilities to Indianapolis, Indiana, two years ago. In early 2010, it's making a multimillion-dollar investment to expand and create up to 100 new jobs in Indiana. The company said the area offers a "favorable business environment and lower total cost of operations, plus a local work force with strong skills in both engineering and manufacturing."

12. Bild Industries Inc., which specializes in business news, directories and market reports, moved to Post Falls, Idaho, from Van Nuys.

13. Bill Miller Engineering, Ltd., suffering under the"hostile business climate" in California and LosAngeles County, moved from Harbor City to Carson City, Nevada .

14. BMC Select has conducted an unusual relocation. The company, which had shifted its headquarters from

Idaho to San Francisco, relocated its H.Q. back to Boise in January 2010. The building materials distributor said that regaining its footing in Boise retained access to high-quality employees while reducing wage and occupancy costs.

15. BPI Labs, which formulates, manufactures, and fills personal care products for the health and beauty industry, relocated from Sacramento to Evanston, Wyoming, a move the company's owner called "very successful . . . . It felt good and I've never looked back."

16. Buck Knives after 62 years in San Diego moved to Post Falls, Idaho.

17. CalPortland Cement has announced in late 2009 closure of its Riverside County plant because of new environmental regulations from a state law (AB 32). The company's CEO wrote, "A cement plant cannot be picked up and moved, but the next new plant probably won't be built in California meaning more good, high-paying manufacturing jobs will be lost to Nevada or China or somewhere."

18. California Casualty Group left San Mateo for Colorado, cutting operating costs to remain competitive.

19. CalStar Products Inc., headquartered in Newark in the San Francisco Bay Area, in January 2010 was

awarded $2.44 million in federal clean energy tax credits. The company said in the future it expects to build additional plants in the Mississippi Valley and the East Coast. In late 2009 CalStar opened a plant in Caledonia, Wisconsin.

20. Checks To-Go moved to Utah where workers' comp rates helped make the troubled company healthier.

21. Chivaroli & Associates, a healthcare-related insurance service based in Westlake Village moved a regional office to Spokane, Washington.

22. CoreSite, A Carlyle Company, is delaying a Santa Clara project while it expands its data center in Reston, Va.

23. Creators Syndicate may flee L.A. because it operates like a "banana republic."

24. Creel Printing Left Costa Mesa for Las Vegas and So Cal loses 60 more jobs.

25. Dassault Falcon looked at building an aircraft services facility in Riverside County but instead located in Reno.

26. DaVita Inc. moved its HQ from Los Angeles to Denver; expects to see millions of dollars in savings over time.

27. Denny,s Corp. - the large restaurant chain once had its headquarters in La Mirada, later in Irvine and then moved to Spartanburg, South Carolina. The company was founded in California and its growth over time created HQ jobs in another state.

28. Digital Domain, the Academy-Award-winning visual effects studio based in Venice placed new studios in Vancouver , British Columbia, and Port St. Lucie, Florida.

29. Ditech, headquartered in Costa Mesa, announced in January 2010 a 269-job cut and is moving most activities to the GMAC Financial Services (parent company) headquarters in Fort Washington, Pennsylvania. In 2007, Ditech relocated some workers from Costa Mesa to Phoenix. A once robust Costa Mesa facility employing hundreds will be down to 20 or 30 workers.

30. DuPont Fabros Technology suspended a $270 million Santa Clara data center project in favor of one in Ashburn, Va.

31. eBay, based in San Jose, will create 450 jobs in Draper, Utah , in a new $334 million operations, customer support and data center.

32. EDMO Distributors, Inc., a world-wide wholesaler of aircraft avionics, test equipment, and pilot supplies,

moved its HQ from Valencia, Calif., to Spokane Valley, Wash. Since, it has built a larger headquarters in the city's Mirabeau Point community complex.

33. Edwards Lifesciences based in Irvine will expand with 1,000 employees not in California but in Draper, Utah .

34. EMRISE Corp. completed its HQ move from Rancho Cucamonga to Eatontown, NJ , in May 2009. The company said the move "will result in additional annualized cost savings of approximately $1 million and facilitate improvements in operating efficiency. . . . The cost savings associated with relocating our corporate headquarters will start immediately. . . The aggregate total of these expense reductions will increase our profitability and cash flow in this and succeeding years and, over time, substantially improve our ability to further reduce our long term debt."

35. Facebook, based in Palo Alto, will expand in a major way in Oregon by locating a custom data center in Prineville. It will be a 147,000-square-foot facility costing $180 million and will employ 200 workers during construction and another 35 full-time once operating in 2011.

36. FallLine Corporation Left Huntington Beach, where they were being "hammered" with multiple governmental regulatory fees, for Reno, Nevada.

37. Fidelity National Financial left Santa Barbara for Florida, spurred by California's "oppressive" business environment.

38. First American Corp., based in Santa Ana, will open a call center in March 2010 not in California but in Phoenix , where it expects to employ about 400 people within two years.

39. Fluor Corp. moved its global headquarters from Aliso Viejo to Irving, Texas, with about 100 employees asked to relocate while the company planned to hire the same number there. In 2006, when Fluor moved into its new headquarters building, a company statement said: "The official dedication had a decidedly Texas theme" as a horseshoe was raised on the building, a time-honored Texas tradition.

40. Foxconn Electronics, a large contract electronics maker, moved some of its Fullerton operations to Dallas.

41. Fuel System Solutions moved its headquarters from Santa Ana to New York.

42. Gregg Industries, owned by Neenah Enterprises Inc. in Wisconsin, closed a 300-employee foundry in El Monte foundry under pressure from the South Coast Air Quality Management District to make $5 million in upgrades. The company didn't want to make

the investment in the difficult economic climate so it decided instead to leave the state.

43. Helix Wind Inc. may move its research and development, engineering, and testing departments from San Diego to "more supportive" Oregon .

44. Hewlett-Packard, HQ'd in Palo Alto, at various times has moved jobs to Tennessee and Texas .

45. Hilton Hotels Corp. in 2009 is moving from its longtime corporate H.Q. in Beverly Hills to a new office in Tysons Corner, Virginia.

46. Hino Motor Manufacturing USA moved from California to Williamstown, West Virginia, in 2007, where it now employs about 100 workers. The company has growth plans to "Raise Hino's presence from medium-/heavy /heavy-duty trucks to all ranges of trucks" and an aggressive program to improve fuel economy and emissions. The company builds trucks under its own brand and also manufactures Toyota-branded vehicles.

47. Intel Corporation, HQ'd in Santa Clara, has chosen to expand operations in neighboring states

48. Intuit of Mountain View created a customer support office (110 people) not in California but in Colorado because of lower operating costs.

49. Intuit placed a data center near Quincy, Washington.

50. Intuit also located Innovative Merchant Solutions LLC in Las Vegas as part of a $1.8 million investment in Nevada.

51. J.C. Penney closed its Sacramento call center and moved the work to five out-of-state centers.

52. Kimmie Candy Co., a manufacturer that was started in 1999, moved from Sacramento to Nevada in 2005. "I really don't have a lot of regrets about moving up to Reno ," said owner Joe Dutra.

53. Klaussner Home Furnishings in closing its La Mirada manufacturing plant will maintain its NC and Iowa operations.

54. Knight Protective Industries moved to Oregon "where 4-day work weeks were permitted by the state" and wanted by the employees.

55. Kulicke & Soffa Industries Inc. announced in February 2010 that it is closing its Irvine plant, laying off 56 people, and will shift the work to Malaysia and Singapore. The facility had been owned by Orthodyne Electronics Corp., which Kulicke & Soffa bought in 2008.

56. LCF Enterprises, which makes specialized high-end amplifiers used by researchers, medical professionals and others, moved from Camarillo, Calif., to Post Falls, Idaho.

57. Lennox Hearth Products Inc. in Orange, Calif, will lay off 71 workers and by March 2010 will transfer the jobs to Nashville and Union City, Tennessee, "to reduce costs and increase operating efficiencies."

58. Lyn-Tron, Inc., a supplier of electronic hardware, moved from Los Angeles to Spokane, Wash. Their website has a rather California(ish) statement: "Our commitment is to maintain a manufacturing environment that is progressive and safe, where our employees are able to achieve their personal objectives, thereby adding to their quality of life and to the community in which they live."

59. Mariah Power, a "green" manufacturer of small wind turbines, moved from California to Nevada and in 2009 teamed up with another company to begin production in Manistee, Michigan.

60. Maxwell America, a boating equipment maker, in February 2010 closed its Santa Ana offices and moved them to Hanover, Md. One reason given was the indirect impact of California environmental regulations. A company official said over the years many California boat builders relocated to the

Midwest and East where they don't face the same restrictions.

61. MiaSolé, based in the Silicon Valley, was reported in January 2010 to be planning a 500,000-square-foot plant, which could be one of the largest solar factories in the United States. The location is not near its in Santa Clara headquarters but in the Atlanta, Georgia, area where its workforce eventually could exceed 1,000. The news came one week after MiaSolé received $101.8 million in federal tax credits.

62. MotorVac Technologies announced in February 2010 that it's leaving Santa Ana for Ontario, Canada. MotorVac's CEO said he "really fought hard to keep MotorVac here, but unfortunately the numbers didn't support it. "The move cuts costs because it's new owner, UView, has its own plant with excess capacity in Canada. "And the general cost of doing business in California is much more expensive."

63. Nissan North America moved its Los Angeles headquarters to Nashville, Tenn.

64. Northrop Grumman by 2011 will relocate its Los Angeles H.Q. to the Washington, DC metro area. It's the last major aerospace company to leave Southern California, the birthplace of the aerospace industry.

65. One2Believe, a specialty religious-toy maker, left California for East Aurora, New York.

66. Patmont Motor Werks, Inc. (GoPed manufacturer), after being hit by California regulators for hundreds of thousands of dollars in small fines even though his company has a stellar safety record, moved to Nevada.

67. Paragon Relocation Resources moved from Rancho Santa Margarita to Irving, Texas.

68. Pixel Magic, headquartered in Toluca Lake, Calif., (Los Angeles metro area), is locating a studio in Lafayette, Louisiana, where it will create 40 new jobs between 2010 and 2013. The company, which provides digital effects for motion pictures and television, said the Louisiana people they were in contact with have an immediate understanding of technology and data handling.

69. Plastic Model Engineering, Inc., a custom plastic injection molder and mold manufacturer, moved from Sylmar, Calif. to the "Inland Northwest," notably Post Falls, Idaho.

70. Precor will stop manufacturing fitness machines in California and re-open in North Carolina.

71. Premier Inc., the largest healthcare alliance in the nation, will move its HQ from San Diego to Charlotte, involving an investment of $17.7 million and adding

300 jobs in North Carolina. The announcement was made Oct. 14, 2009.

72. Pro Cal of South Gate, in Los Angeles County, a unit of Myers Industries, expanded its Sparks, Nev., operations to become the company's primary West Coast production and distribution facility. Pro Cal is a plastics manufacturer of nursery containers and a big recycler.

73. Race Track Chaplaincy of America started 2010 by shifting its headquarters from Los Angeles to Lexington, Kentucky. The non-profit group said it had wanted to relocate from the Hollywood Park Race Track for several reasons, one of which is the significant cost of doing business on the West Coast.

74. Red Truck Fire & Safety Company left Fresno for Minden, Nevada in 2007 because of California's myriad fees and regulations that meant "death by thousand cuts."

75. SAIC will move its headquarters east, from San Diego to McLean, Virginia, which the Washington Post called "Another Coup for Area." The announcement was made Sept. 24, 2009; it is unclear how many employees will move east in 2009 and 2010.

76. Scale Computing, a data-storage developer and manufacturer, is leaving Silicon Valley for Indiana.

77. Schott Solar Inc. will close its sales and customer service office in Roseville and will relocate the office to Albuquerque, NM.

78. SimpleTech transferred its manufacturing work from Santa Ana to Asia more than a year ago.

79. Smiley Industries, an aerospace manufacturer, moved to Phoenix, where productivity improved.

80. Solaicx, based in the Silicon Valley, said in early 2010 that it will expand its manufacturing plant in Portland , Oregon. Solaicx received $18.2 million in federal tax credits as part of Washington's efforts to advance green energy.

81. SolarWorld, a maker of solar technology founded in Camarillo, consolidated manufacturing in Oregon after that state offered property tax abatement and business energy tax credits. The company will employ about 1,000 in Oregon by 2011

82. Special Devices Inc. brought 250 jobs to Mesa , Arizona, from Moorpark, Calif.

83. StarKist headquarters is leaving San Francisco for Pittsburgh, Pa.

84. Stasis Engineering moved from Sonoma County to West Virginia, a "friendlier business climate."

85. Stata Corp., which specializes in data analysis and statistical software, moved from Santa Monica, California to College Station, Texas.

86. Tapmatic, a metalworking firm whose owners were "fed up with the onerous business environment," moved from Orange County, California to Post Falls in northern Idaho.

87. Teledesic moved to Washington state in anticipation of better capital gains.

88. Telmar Network Technology Inc. moved from Irvine to Plano, Texas, consolidating some 150 workers there.

89. Terremark postponed a Santa Clara project earlier this year to invest $50 million in a Culpeper, Va. project.

90. Terumo Cardiovascular Systems is moving R&D from OC to Ann Arbor, Michigan, involving 65 jobs and $3.5 million in investments.

91. Toyota will stop making cars in Fremont, will idle 4,700 workers, and move work to Canada and San Antonio, Texas.

92. True Games Interactive Inc. will its H.Q. from Irvine to Austin, Texas, where it expects to have about 60 workers by the middle of 2010.

93. TTM Technologies will leave L.A. & Hayward and move to other states and China to achieve big cost savings.

94. Twentieth Century Props of L.A. has gone out of business as film-making has moved to lower-cost states

95. Understand.com <http://understand.com/> moved from the San Francisco Bay Area to Reno, a loss for California in that the company is a leader in web-based patient education content and shows strong growth. The company was named 2007 Innovator of the Year by a Northern publication and the company's founder and received a media and Reno-Tahoe Young Professionals Network "20 Under 40" award and was selected as a 20/20 Business Visionary by Nevada Business Magazine.

96. US Airways is realigning operations and California is no longer considered part of its "core." The airline is closing its John Wayne Airport maintenance station and in early 2010 will redistribute the mechanics across its system.

97. US Press shifted work from Los Angeles and San Diego to Portland, "where union rules were almost rational."

98. USAA Insurance closed its 625-person Sacramento campus in favor of other states.

99. Yahoo opened a data center in Quincy, Washington , a community that now hopes to land high-tech manufacturing.

The list will grow as Sacramento considers more measures that will increase corporate taxes, increase workers' comp costs, increase regulatory reporting requirements (along with higher fines for minor infractions), increase gasoline and diesel-fuel taxes, increase water rates, increase electric-power rates, and increase assorted fees that will cause services to become more expensive.

Businesses don't move because they like to. They move to stay in business and California doesn't seem to be the place to stay in business.

Governor elect - Jerry Brown - said that California needed jobs. But his previous policies did not allow for expansion. How he plans to increase the jobs base will be interesting to watch.
The Government continues to state that the economy is righting itself and there is nothing to worry about. DON'T BELIEVE IT! This country is in dire straights

and it will take a great deal of time to "right itself". If we're not too late to start - that is.

All governments, federal, state and local have mismanaged their fiduciary duties and allowed each to bankrupt themselves. There are very few governing bodies that don't fall into this category. Even the small City of Bell, California felt the sting of corruption.

Eight current and former Bell, California, city officials arrested and charged with misappropriation of funds and making or receiving illegal loans demonstrated "corruption on steroids," the Los Angeles County district attorney said.

The charges allege the officials misappropriated more than $5.5 million, including being paid for phantom meetings, District Attorney Steve Cooley said at a news conference.

High salaries paid to officials of the city sparked local outrage and national attention when they came to light in July. Bell City Manager Robert Rizzo, Police Chief Randy Adams and Assistant City Manager Angela Spaccia resigned after media reports that they were making several hundred thousand dollars a year each. Adams was not charged, Cooley said.
Not only are these officials, and others like them, bankrupting the hand that feeds them, but they are morally bankrupt as well. What would possess

anyone in a city of 36,000 believe they are worth $800,000 a year?

I'm sorry to report that I profile quite a bit. If you saw the mug shots of these "officials" you also would call them corrupt. They just look like the kind to stick their hand in the cookie jar and dare anyone to squeal. After seeing their "shots" why would you have voted for them in the first place? At least BO has a "slick Willy" appearance instead of Al Capone.

Here's a profile test:

Maddening! Absolutely No Profiling!

Pause a moment, reflect back, and take the following multiple choice test. These events are actual events from history..

They really happened! Do you remember?

HERE'S THE TEST

1. 1968   Bobby Kennedy was shot and killed by: a.. Superman   b. Jay Leno   c. Harry Potter   d. A Muslim male extremist between the ages of 17 and 40

2. In 1972 at the Munich Olympics, athletes were kidnapped and massacred by: a. Olga Corbett   b.

Sitting Bull   c.   Arnold Schwarzenegger   d.   Muslim male extremists mostly between the ages of 17 and 40

3. In 1979, the US embassy in Iran was taken over by: a. Lost Norwegians   b. Elvis   c. A tour bus full of 80-year-old women   d Muslim male extremists mostly between the ages of 17 and 40

4. During the 1980's a number of Americans were kidnapped in Lebanon   by: a. John Dillinger b. The King of Sweden c. The Boy Scouts d. Muslim male extremists mostly between the ages of 17 and 40

5. In 1983, the US Marine barracks in Beirut was blown up by: a. A pizza delivery boy b. Pee Wee Herman   c..   Geraldo Rivera d. Muslim male extremists mostly between the ages of 17 and 40

6. In 1985 the cruise ship Achille Lauro was hijacked and a 70 year old American passenger was murdered and thrown overboard in his wheelchair by: a. The Smurfs b. Davey Jones c. The Little Mermaid d. Muslim male extremists mostly between the ages of 17 and 40

7. In 1985 TWA flight 847 was hijacked at Athens, and a US Navy diver trying to rescue passengers was murdered by: a. Captain Kidd b. Charles Lindberg c. Mother Teresa d. Muslim male extremists mostly between the ages of 17 and 40

8. In 1988, Pan Am Flight 103 was bombed by: a. Scooby Doo b. The Tooth Fairy c. The Sundance Kid d. Muslim male extremists mostly between the ages of 17 and 40

9. In 1993 the World Trade Center was bombed the first time by: a. Richard Simmons b. Grandma Moses c. Michael Jordan d. Muslim male extremists mostly between the ages of 17 and 40

10. In 1998, the US embassies in Kenya and Tanzania were bombed by: a. Mr. Rogers b. Hillary Clinton, to distract attention from Wild Bill c. The World Wrestling Federation d. Muslim male extremists mostly between the ages of 17 and 40

11. On 9/11/01, four airliners were hijacked; two were used as missiles to take out the World Trade Centers and of the remaining two, one crashed into the US Pentagon and the other was diverted and crashed by the passengers. Thousands of people were killed by: a. Bugs Bunny, Wiley E. Coyote, Daffy Duck and Elmer Fudd b. The Supreme Court of Florida c. Mr

Bean d. Muslim male extremists mostly between the ages of 17 and 40

12. In   2002 the United States fought a war in Afghanistan   against: a. Enron b. The Lutheran Church   c. The   NFL   d. Muslim male extremists mostly between the ages of 17 and 40

13. In 2002 reporter Daniel Pearl was kidnapped and murdered   by: a. Bonnie and Clyde   b. Captain Kangaroo c. Billy Graham d. Muslim male extremists mostly between the ages of 17 and 40

No, I really don't see a pattern here to justify profiling, do you? So, to ensure we Americans never offend anyone, particularly fanatics intent   on killing us, airport security screeners will no longer be allowed to profile certain people.   They must conduct random searches of   80-year-old women, little kids,   airline pilots with proper   identification,   secret agents who are members of the President's   security detail, 85-year old Congressmen with metal hips, and Medal of Honor winner and former Governor Joe Foss, but leave Muslim Males   between the ages 17 and 40 alone lest they be guilty of profiling.

Foot note: Fort Hood Texas ......another Muslim 39 years old killed 13 people and wounded 30 some odd others...

Does this fit the profile?

NOW OUR   COMMANDER-IN-CHIEF IS TELLING EVERYONE THAT THE YOUNG MUSLIM THAT ATTEMPTED TO BLOW UP A NORTHWEST/DELTA JET AS IT APPROACHED DETROIT ON CHRISTMAS DAY WAS (QUOTE) "AN ISOLATED INCIDENT".

ARE YOU KIDDING!!!

"PLEASE DON'T PEE ON MY LEG AND TELL ME IT'S RAINING."

What happens in Washington is slightly more sophisticated.   This is an example of how our Senators work.   This happens to tell about BO as a Senator:

More on the Sherrod story...
The tables turn quickly sometimes......

Andrew Breitbart is a media genius?

He proved it originally with his brilliant handling of the ACORN 'hooker' scandal which he skillfully manipulated so that the corrupt media was forced, against its will, to broadcast corruption in one of Obama's most powerful political support groups. But Breitbart's handing of that affair is nothing compared to his brilliant manipulation of the Shirley Sherrod 'white farmer' scandal.

It all began last Monday, July 22, 2010. As the country watched in horror, Breitbart released a snippet of a tape on his "Big Government" website which showed an obscure black female official of the Dept. of Agriculture laughing to a roomful of NAACP members about how she'd discriminated against a destitute white farmer and refused to give him the financial aid he desperately needed. As she smirked to the room, she'd sent him instead to a white lawyer – 'one of his own kind' – for help. The black woman was Shirley Sherrod – and almost immediately she became the center of a firestorm of controversy which exploded throughout the country. Within a day of the release of that infamous tape, the head of the Dept. of Agriculture, spurred on by Obama, demanded – and received – Sherrod's resignation. Breitbart had won.

But then seemingly Breitbart's actions began to explode in his face. As Sherrod screamed in protest, FOX News released the entire text of her speech last March to the NAACP. And there on tape Sherrod was shown supposedly repenting of her racism against a white farmer and instead championing his fight to win funds to keep his farm afloat. Within hours of that entire tape being revealed, the entire world turned against Andrew Breitbart. Conservatives throughout the country were enraged that he'd endangered their reputations by releasing a 'doctored' tape. Breitbart, they thundered, had dealt a fatal blow to the conservative media. I confess that I also was horrified at what I saw as the clumsiness and stupidity of Breitbart in 'doctoring' a tape to make a supposedly innocent woman look guilty. But now I discover I have been as guilty of haste to judgment of Breitbart as the Dept. of Agriculture was of Ms. Sherrod.

Only now am I realizing the real purpose for Breitbart's release of that tape snippet. It was to allow him to cunningly trick the media into exposing one of the most shocking examples of corruption in the federal government – a little known legal case called "Pigford v. Glickman".

April 23 2010 - http://deltafarmpress.com/legislative/pigford-glickman-update-0423/

CASE: http://lw.bna.com/lw/19981020/971978.htm

http://pajamasmedia.com/zombie/2010/07/27/pigford-v-glickman-86000-claims-from-39697-total-farmers/?singlepage=true

"In 1997, 400 African-American farmers sued the United States Department of Agriculture, alleging that they had been unfairly denied USDA loans due to racial discrimination during the period 1983 to 1997." The case was entitled "Pigford v. Glickman" and in 1999, the black farmers won their case. The government agreed to pay each of them as much as

$50,000 to settle their claims.

But then on February 23 of this year, something shocking happened in relation to that original judgment. In total silence, the USDA agreed to release more funds to "Pigford". The amount was a staggering $1.25 billion. This was because the original number of plaintiffs – 400 black farmers – had now swollen in a class action suit to include a total of 86,000 black farmers throughout America.

There was only one teensy problem. The United States of America doesn't have 86,000 black farmers. According to accurate and totally verified census data, the total number of black farmers throughout America is only 39,697. Oops.

Well, gosh – how on earth did 39,697 explode into 86,000 claims? And how did $50,000 explode into $1.25 billion? Well, folks, you'll just have to ask the woman who not only spearheaded this case because of her position in 1997 at the "Rural Development Leadership Network" but whose family received the highest single payout (approximately $13 million) from that action – Shirley Sherrod. Oops again.

http://beforeitsnews.com/story/110/024/
Is_There_More_to_Sherrods_Dismissal.html

Yes, folks. It appears that Ms. Sherrod had just unwittingly exposed herself as the perpetrator of one of the biggest fraud claims in the United States – a fraud enabled solely because she screamed racism at the government and cowed them into submission. And it gets even more interesting. Ms. Sherrod has also exposed the person who aided and abetted her in this race fraud. As it turns out, the original judgment of "Pigford v. Glickman" in 1999 only applied to a total of 16,000 black farmers. But in 2008, a junior Senator got a law passed to reopen the case and allow more black farmers to sue for funds. The Senator was Barack Obama.

Because this law was passed in dead silence and because the woman responsible for spearheading it was an obscure USDA official, American taxpayers did not realize that they had just been forced in the midst of a worldwide depression to pay out more than $1.25 billion to settle a race claim.

But Breitbart knew. And on July 22, 2010, he cleverly laid a trap which Sherrod – and Obama – stumbled headfirst into which has now resulted in the entire world discovering the existence of this corrupt financial judgment. Yes, folks – Breitbart is a genius.

As for Ms. Sherrod? Well, she's discovered too late that her cry of 'racism' to the media which was intended to throw the spotlight on Breitbart has instead thrown that spotlight on herself – and her corruption. Sherrod has vanished from public view. Her 'pigs', it seems, have come home to roost. Oink!

Not only is Senator BO at fault for upping the ante, but the judges in the case are also at fault for allowing this to happen. WHAT THE HELL IS WRONG WITH PEOPLE???

We have suffered through many fools recently and so many of them are still in Washington. I received an email letter to President BO from a number of Representatives chiding him on several speeches he recently gave. They are members of the Congressional Prayer Caucus and they take issue with him regarding our national motto. BO says its *E pluribus unium* when it is actually; In God We Trust. This was signed into law in 1956.

BO also screwed up when he stated from the Declaration of Independence that we have inalienable rights but failed to state where those rights came from. It is very clear that those rights come from God, our creator, but BO cannot acknowledge God since he believes that Mohammed is his god.

This man is an Islamic creature and we elected him President of the United States of America. I say again - "WHAT THE HELL IS WRONG WITH PEOPLE???

These are very troubling times.

GOD BLESS AMERICA & CANADA

These are troubling times.

This was written by a woman born in Egypt as a Muslim. This is not heresy, and it will scare you.

Joys of Muslim Women by Nonie Darwish

In the Muslim faith a Muslim man can marry a child as young as 7 years old, consummating the marriage by 9. The dowry is given to the family in exchange for the woman (who becomes his slave) and for the purchase of the private parts of the woman, to use her as a toy

To prove rape, the woman must have (4) male witnesses. Often after a woman has been raped. The family has the right to execute her (an honor killing) to restore the honor of the family. Husbands can beat their wives 'at will' and the man does not have to say why he has beaten her.

The husband is permitted to have 4 wives and a temporary wife for an hour (prostitute) at his discretion.

The Shariah Muslim law controls the private as well as the public life of the woman.

In the Western World (America) Muslim men are starting to demand Shariah Law so the wife can not obtain a divorce and he can have full and complete control of her. It is amazing and alarming how many of our sisters and daughters attending US and Canadian Universities are now marrying Muslim men and submitting themselves and their children unsuspectingly to the Shariah law.

By passing this on, enlightened US and Canadian women may avoid becoming a slave under Shariah Law.

Ripping the West in Two. Author and lecturer Nonie Darwish says the goal of radical Islamists is to impose Shariah law on the world, ripping Western law and liberty in two.

She recently authored the book, Cruel and Usual Punishment: The Terrifying Global Implications of Islamic Law.

Darwish was born in Cairo and spent her childhood in Egypt and Gaza before immigrating to the US in 1978, when she was eight years old. Her father died while leading covert attacks on Israel . He was a high-ranking Egyptian military officer stationed with his family in Gaza .

When he died, he was considered a "shahid," a martyr for jihad. His posthumous status earned Nonie and her family an elevated position in Muslim society.

But Darwish developed a skeptical eye at an early age. She questioned her own Muslim culture and upbringing. She converted to Christianity after hearing a Christian preacher on television.

In her latest book, Darwish warns about creeping sharia law - what it is, what it means, and how it is manifested in Islamic countries.

For the West, she says radical Islamists are working to impose sharia on the world. If that happens, Western civilization will be destroyed. Westerners generally assume all religions encourage a respect for the dignity of each individual. Islamic law (Sharia) teaches that non-Muslims should be subjugated or killed in this world.

Peace and prosperity for one's children is not as important as assuring that Islamic law rules everywhere in the Middle East and eventually in the world.

While Westerners tend to think that all religions encourage some form of the golden rule, Sharia teaches two systems of ethics - one for Muslims and another for non-Muslims. Building on tribal practices of the seventh century, Sharia encourages the side of humanity that wants to take from and subjugate others.

While Westerners tend to think in terms of religious people developing a personal understanding of and relationship with God, Sharia advocates executing people who ask difficult questions that could be interpreted as criticism.

It's hard to imagine, that in this day and age, Islamic scholars agree that those who criticize Islam or choose to stop being Muslim should be executed. Sadly, while talk of an Islamic reformation is common and even assumed by many in the West, such murmurings in the Middle East are silenced through intimidation.

While Westerners are accustomed to an increase in religious tolerance over time, Darwish explains how petro dollars are being used to grow an extremely intolerant form of political Islam in her native Egypt and elsewhere.

In twenty years there will be enough Muslim voters in the U.S. and Canada to elect the President or Prime Minister by themselves! Rest assured they will do so... You can look at how they have taken over several towns in the USA and Canada, Dearborn Mich. is one, Brampton, Ontario is another and there are others... As of 10/10 News report: Paterson, N.J. is the 2nd largest Islamic city in the USA!

I think everyone in the U.S. and Canada should be required to read this, but with the ACLU, there is no way this will be widely publicized, unless each of us sends it on!

It is too bad that so many are disillusioned with life and Christianity to accept Muslims as peaceful.. some may be, but they have an army that is willing to shed blood in the name of Islam.. the peaceful support the warriors with their finances and own kind of patriotism to their religion. While the US and Canada are getting rid of Christianity from all public sites and erasing God from the lives of children the Muslims are planning a great jihad on the US and Canada.

I hope that this didn't scare you too bad. We still have some hope, but nothing has happened as yet. Maybe the judges are afraid of BO???

Barack Obama May Be In Deep Trouble..

Chief Justice John Roberts, U.S. Supreme Court.

According to sources who watch the inner workings of the federal government, a smack down of Barack Obama by the U.S. Supreme Court may be inevitable ever since Obama assumed the office of President, critics have hammered him on a number of Constitutional issues.

Critics have complained that much, if not all of Obama's major initiatives run headlong into Constitutional roadblocks on the power of the federal government. Obama certainly did not help himself in the eyes of the Court when he used the venue of the State of the Union address early in the year to publicly flog the Court over its ruling that the First Amendment grants the right to various organizations to run political ads during the time of an election.

The tongue-lashing clearly did not sit well with the Court, as demonstrated by Justice Sam Alito, who publicly shook his head and stated under his breath, 'That's not true,'when Obama told a flat-out lie concerning the Court's ruling.

As it has turned out, this was a watershed moment in the relationship between the executive and the judicial branches of the federal government. Obama publicly declared war on the court, even as he blatantly continued to propose legislation that flies in the face of every known Constitutional principle upon which this nation has stood for over 200 years.

Obama has even identified Chief Justice John Roberts as his number one enemy, that is, apart from Fox News and Rush Limbaugh, Beck, Hannity, and so on.

And it is no accident that the one swing-vote on the court, Justice Anthony Kennedy, stated recently that he has no intention of retiring until 'Obama is gone.'

Apparently, the Court has had enough.

The Roberts Court has signaled, in a very subtle manner, of course, that it intends to address the issues about which Obama critics have been screaming to high heaven.

A ruling against Obama on any one of these important issues could potentially cripple the Administration.

Such a thing would be long overdue.

First, there is ObamaCare, which violates the Constitutional principle barring the federal government from forcing citizens to purchase something. And no, this is not the same thing as states requiring drivers to purchase car insurance, as some of the intellectually impaired claim.

The Constitution limits FEDERAL government, not state governments, from such things, and further, not everyone has to drive, and thus, a citizen could opt not to purchase car insurance by simply deciding not to drive a vehicle.

In the ObamaCare world, however, no citizen can 'opt out.'

Second, sources state that the Roberts court has quietly accepted information concerning discrepancies in Obama's history that raise serious questions about his eligibility for the office of President.

The charge goes far beyond the birth certificate issue. This information involves possible fraudulent use of a Social Security number in Connecticut, while Obama was a high school student in Hawaii.

And that is only the tip of the iceberg.

Third, several cases involving possible criminal activity, conflicts of interest, and pay-for-play cronyism could potentially land many Administration officials, if not Obama himself, in hot water with the Court.

Frankly, in the years this writer has observed politics, nothing comes close to comparing with the rampant corruption of this Administration, not even during the Nixon years.

Nixon and the Watergate conspirators look like choirboys compared to the jokers that populate this Administration.

In addition, the Court will eventually be forced to rule on the dreadful decision of the Obama DOJ suing the state of Arizona.

That, too, could send the Obama doctrine of open borders to an early grave, given that the Administration refuses to enforce federal law on illegal aliens.

And finally, the biggie that could potentially send the entire house of cards tumbling in a free-fall is the latest revelation concerning the Obama-Holder Department of Justice and its refusal to pursue the New Black Panther Party.

The group was caught on tape committing felonies by attempting to intimidate Caucasian voters into staying away from the polls.

A whistle-blower who resigned from the DOJ is now charging Holder with the deliberate refusal to pursue cases against Blacks, particularly those who are involved in radical hate- groups, such as the New Black Panthers, who have been caught on tape calling for the murder of white people and their babies.

This one is a biggie that could send the entire Administration crumbling--that is, if the Justices have the guts to draw a line in the sand at the Constitution and the Bill of Rights.

For those that really believe that BO is doing a good job - read on. You have to admit that BO is slowly turning the USA into a Socialistic country. He promises that he won't raise taxes on the middle class, but you have to read where the socialistic countries in Europe are regarding taxes. This is enough to curl your hair - if you have any left after reading so far:

Current European tax rates:

United Kingdom
  Income Tax: 50%
    VAT: 17.5% TOTAL: 67.5%

France
  Income Tax: 40%
    VAT: 19.6% TOTAL: 59.6%

Greece
  Income Tax: 40%
    VAT: 25%   TOTAL: 65%

Spain
  Income Tax: 45%
    VAT: 16%   TOTAL: 61%

Portugal
  Income Tax: 42%
    VAT: 20%   TOTAL: 62%

Sweden
Income Tax: 55%
VAT: 25%   TOTAL: 80%

Norway
Income Tax: 54.3%
VAT: 25%   TOTAL: 79.3%

Netherlands
Income Tax: 52%
VAT: 19%   TOTAL: 71%

Denmark
Income Tax: 58%
VAT: 25%   TOTAL: 83%

Finland
Income Tax: 53%
VAT: 22%   TOTAL: 75%

If you've started to wonder what the real costs of socialism are going to be, once the full program in these United States hits your wallet, take a look at the table. As you digest these mind-boggling figures, keep in mind that in spite of these astronomical tax rates, these countries are still not financing their social welfare programs exclusively from tax revenues! They are deeply mired in public debt of gargantuan proportions. Greece has reached the point where its debt is so huge it is in imminent danger of defaulting. That is the reason the European economic community has intervened to bail them out. If you're following the financial news, you know Spain and Portugal are right behind Greece.

The United States is now heading right down the same path. The VAT tax in the table is the national sales tax that Europeans pay. Stay tuned because that is exactly what you can expect to see the administration proposing after the fall elections. The initial percentage in the United States isn't going to be anywhere near the outrageous numbers you now see in Europe. Guess what, the current outrageous numbers in Europe didn't start out as outrageous either. They started out as minuscule - right around the 1% or 2% where they will start out in the United States. Magically however, they ran up over the years to where they are now. Expect the same thing here.

It is the notion that with hard work and perseverance, anybody can get ahead economically here. Do you think that can ever happen with tax rates between 60% and 80%? Think again. With the government taking that percentage of your money, your life will be exactly like life in Europe. You pay dearly to buy a home. You might not want a car with it's taxes for registration and gas (the governor of Colorado recently put a fee...another name for a tax....on our car registration. I paid over $500 to register my car last month.) You would hope some of that government $$$s go to the state universities because you will never afford to send your children to college without it. Let's not shuffle the battle cry of the socialists under the rug either. It's always the same cry. Equalize income. Spread the wealth to the poor (whoever they are). Level the economic playing field. Accomplish that and everything will be rosy. BS....free health care my butt!

It's time to take a really hard look at reality. Greece is a perfect example. Despite the socialism system that has ruled this country for decades, with a 65% tax rate, they are drowning in public debt, would have defaulted without hundreds of billions in bailout money, and still. . . .20% of their population lives in poverty. What has all that socialism money bought, besides ultimate power for the politicians running the show? Do you think these people are "free"? They're not. They are slaves to their economic "system."

I firmly believe if our government continues to "redistribute" our economic system, this is where we are going.

The Good News

According to sources who watch the inner workings of the federal government, a smack down of Barack Obama by the U.S. Supreme Court may be inevitable.

Ever since Obama assumed the office of President, critics have hammered him on a number of Constitutional issues. Critics have complained that much if not all of Obama's major initiatives run headlong into Constitutional roadblocks on the power of the federal government.

Obama certainly did not help himself in the eyes of the Court when he used the venue of the State of the Union address early in the year to publicly flog the Court over its ruling that the First Amendment grants the right to various organizations to run political ads during the time of an election.

The tongue-lashing clearly did not sit well with the Court, as demonstrated by Justice Sam Alito, who publicly shook his head and stated under his breath, 'That's not true,' when Obama told a flat-out lie concerning the Court's ruling. As it has turned out, this was a watershed moment in the relationship between the executive and the judicial branches of the federal government. Obama publicly declared war on the court, even as he blatantly continued to propose legislation that flies in the face of every known Constitutional principle upon which this nation has stood for over 200 years.

Obama has even identified Chief Justice John Robert s as his number one enemy, that is, apart from Fox News and Rush Limbaugh. And it is no accident that the one swing-vote on the court, Justice Anthony Kennedy, stated recently that he has no intention of retiring until 'Obama is gone.'

Apparently, the Court has had enough. The Robert s Court has signaled, in a very subtle manner, of course, that it intends to address the issues about which Obama critics have been screaming to high heaven. A ruling against Obama on any one of these important issues could potentially cripple the Administration. Such a thing would be long overdue.

First, there is ObamaCare, which violates the Constitutional principle barring the federal government from forcing citizens to purchase something. And no, this is not the same thing as states requiring drivers to purchase car insurance, as some of the intellectually-impaired claim. The Constitution limits FEDERAL government, not state governments, from such things, and further, not everyone has to drive, and thus, a citizen could opt not to purchase car insurance by simply deciding not to drive a vehicle. In the ObamaCare world, however, no citizen can 'opt out.'

Second, sources state that the Robert s court has quietly accepted information concerning discrepancies in Obama's history that raise serious questions about his eligibility for the office of President. The charge goes far beyond the birth certificate issue. This information involves possible fraudulent use of a Social Security number in Connecticut , while Obama was a high school student in Hawaii . And that is only the tip of the iceberg.

Third, several cases involving possible criminal activity, conflicts of interest, and pay-for-play cronyism could potentially land many Administration officials, if not the President himself, in hot water with the Court. Frankly, in the years this writer has observed politics, nothing comes close to comparing with the rampant corruption of this Administration, not even during the Nixon years. Nixon and the Watergate conspirators look like choirboys compared to the jokers that populate this Administration.

In addition, the Court will eventually be forced to rule on the dreadful decision of the Obama DOJ to sue the state of Arizona . That, too, could send the Obama doctrine of open borders to an early grave, given that the Administration refuses to enforce federal law on illegal aliens.

And finally, the biggie that could potentially send the entire house of cards tumbling in a free-fall is the latest revelation concerning the Obama-Holder

Department of Justice and its refusal to pursue the New Black Panther Party. The group is caught on tape committing felonies by attempting to intimidate Caucasian voters into staying away from the polls.

A whistle-blower who resigned from the DOJ is now charging Holder with the deliberate refusal to pursue cases against Blacks, particularly those who are involved in radical hate-groups, such as the New Black Panthers, who have been caught on tape calling for the murder of white people and their babies.

This one is a biggie that could send the entire Administration crumbling--that is, if the Justices have the guts to draw a line in the sand at the Constitution and the Bill of Rights.

Finally we need to hear again what a dysfunctional person BO really is. The following are some comments prior to his election and, sadly, he was elected anyway:

WAS NOBODY LISTENING?
The following is a narrative taken from a 2008 Sunday morning televised "Meet The Press'. The author (Dale Lindsborg) is employed by none other than the very liberal Washington Post!!

From Sunday's 07 Sept. 2008   11:48:04 EST, Televised "Meet the Press" THE

THEN Senator Obama was asked about his stance on the American Flag.

General Bill Ginn' USAF (ret.) asked Obama to explain WHY he doesn't follow protocol when the National Anthem is played. The General stated to Obama that according to the United States Code, Title 36, Chapter 10, Sec. 171...During rendition of the national anthem, when the flag is displayed, all present (except those in uniform) are expected to stand at attention facing the flag with the right hand over the heart. Or, at the very least, "Stand and Face It".

NOW GET THIS!! - - - - -

'Senator' Obama replied:
"As I've said about the flag pin, I don't want to be perceived as taking sides". "There are a lot of people in the world to whom the American flag is a symbol of oppression.." "The anthem itself conveys a war-like message. You know, the bombs bursting in air and all that sort of thing."
(ARE YOU READY FOR THIS???)

Obama continued: "The National Anthem should be 'swapped' for something less parochial and less bellicose. I like the song 'I'd Like To Teach the World To Sing'. If that were our anthem, then, I might salute it. In my opinion, we should consider reinventing our National Anthem as well as 'redesign' our Flag to better offer our enemies hope and love. It's my intention, if elected, to disarm America to the level of acceptance to our Middle East Brethren. If we, as a Nation of waring people, conduct ourselves like the nations of Islam, where peace prevails - - - perhaps a state or period of mutual accord could exist between our governments."

When I become President, I will seek a pact of agreement to end hostilities between those who have been at war or in a state of enmity, and a freedom from disquieting oppressive thoughts. We as a Nation, have placed upon the nations of Islam, an unfair injustice which is WHY my wife disrespects the Flag and she and I have attended several flag burning ceremonies in the past".

"Of course now, I have found myself about to become the President of the United States and I have put my hatred aside. I will use my power to bring CHANGE to this Nation, and offer the people a new path..My wife and I look forward to becoming our Country's First black Family.

Indeed, CHANGE is about to overwhelm the United States of America "
WHAAAAAAAT, the Hell is that!!!
Yes, you read it right.
I, for one, am speechless!!!

Dale Lindsborg , Washington Post

The Change we Need

Sarah Palin is as close to a Ronald Reagan as we are going to get. This country has lost its way again and only someone as strong as a Ronald Reagan will bring it back.

She has more experience than BO ever had. She isn't afraid to stand up to the world and let them know that the USA is here to stay. She isn't afraid to wear the Red, White and Blue on her sleeve and salute the flag or wear a flag pin. She is proud of America and wouldn't bow to any foreigner.

She believes in saving money, balancing the budget, fighting our foes and helping our friends. This is something that the present administration knows very little about.

For those Republicans that oppose her, wake up. We don't want the same old way of doing things to continue. There really isn't much difference between the major parties anymore. To put some of the "has beens" back in office would be like believing that Jerry Brown will govern California differently than he did 20+ years ago. Remember that doing the same thing over and over and expecting different results is really STUPID.

Lets get a little more background on Sarah as Governor of Alaska and Michelle as First Lady.

Very interesting facts on two very different ladies.

By Dewie Whetsell, Alaskan Fisherman. As posted in comments on Greta's article referencing the MOVEON ad about Sarah Palin.

The last 45 of my 66 years I've spent in a commercial fishing town in Alaska . I understand Alaska politics but never understood national politics well until this last year. Here's the breaking point: Neither side of the Palin controversy gets it. It's not about persona, style, rhetoric, it's about doing things. Even Palin supporters never mention the things that I'm about to mention here.

1. Democrats forget when Palin was the Darling of the Democrats, because as soon as Palin took the Governor's office away from a fellow Republican and tough SOB, Frank Murkowski, she tore into the Republican's "Corrupt Bastards Club" (CBC) and sent them packing. Many of them are now residing in State housing and wearing orange jump suits The Democrats reacted by skipping around the yard, throwing confetti and singing, "la la la la" (well, you know how they are). Name another governor in this country that has ever done anything similar.

2. Now with the CBC gone, there were fewer Alaskan politicians to protect the huge, giant oil companies here. So she constructed and enacted a new system of splitting the oil profits called "ACES." Exxon (the biggest corporation in the world) protested and Sarah told them, "don't let the door hit you in the stern on your way out." They stayed, and Alaska residents went from being merely wealthy to being filthy rich. Of course, the other huge   international oil companies meekly fell in line. Again, give me the name of any other governor in the country that has done anything similar.

3. The other thing she did when she walked into the governor's office is she got the list of State requests for federal funding for projects, known as "pork." She went through the list, took 85% of them and placed them in the "when-hell-freezes-over" stack. She let locals know that if we need something built, we'll pay

for it ourselves. Maybe she figured she could use the money she got from selling the previous governor's jet because it was extravagant. Maybe she could use the money she saved by dismissing the governor's cook (remarking that she could cook for her own family), giving back the State vehicle issued to her, maintaining that she already had a car, and dismissing her State-provided security force (never mentioning - I imagine - that she's packing heat herself). I'm still waiting to hear the names of those other governors.

4. Now, even with her much-ridiculed "gosh and golly" mannerism, she also managed to put together a totally new approach to getting a natural gas pipeline built which will be the biggest private construction project in the history of North America. No one else could do it although they tried. If that doesn't impress you, then you're trying too hard to be unimpressed while watching her do things like this while baking up a batch of brownies with her other hand.

5. For 30 years, Exxon held a lease to do exploratory drilling at a place called Point Thompson. They made excuses the entire time why they couldn't start drilling. In truth they were holding it like an investment. No governor for 30 years could make them get started. Then, she told them she was revoking their lease and kicking them out. They protested and threatened court action. She shrugged and reminded them that she knew the way to the court house. Alaska won again.

6. President Obama wants the nation to be on 25% renewable resources for electricity by 2025. Sarah went to the legislature and submitted her plan for Alaska to be at 50% renewable by 2025. We are already at 25%. I can give you more specifics about things done, as opposed to style and persona. Everybody wants to be cool, sound cool, look cool. But that's just a cover-up. I'm still waiting to hear from liberals the names of other governors who can match what mine has done in two and a half years. I won't be holding my breath.

By the way, she was content to return to Alaska after the national election and go to work, but the haters wouldn't let her. Now these adolescent screechers are obviously not scuba divers. And no one ever told them what happens when you continually jab and pester a barracuda. Without warning, it will spin around and tear your face off. Shoulda known better.

You have just read the truth about Sarah Palin that sends the media, along with the Democrat party, into a wild uncontrolled frenzy to discredit her. I guess they are only interested in skirt chasers, dishonesty, immoral people, liars, womanizers, murderers, and bitter ex-presidents' wives. So "You go, Girl." I only wish the men in Washington had your guts, determination, honesty, and morals. I rest my case. Only FOOLS listen to the biased media. NOW If you've read this far ....now, open your eyes..........

First Lady Michelle Obama's Servant List and Pay Scale

TheFirst Lady Requires More Than Twenty Attendants (Thats 22 Attendants to be exact)

1. $172,200 - Sher, Susan (Chief Of Staff)
2. $140,000 - Frye, Jocelyn C. (Deputy Assistant to the President and Director of Policy And Projects For The First Lady)
3. $113,000 - Rogers, Desiree G. (Special Assistant to the President and White House Social Secretary) Resigned recently due to impropriety scandal.
4. $102,000 - Johnston, Camille Y. (Special Assistant to the President and Director of Communications for the First Lady)
5. $100,000 - Winter, Melissa E. (Special Assistant to the President and Deputy Chief Of Staff to the First Lady)
6. $90,000 - Medina , David S. (Deputy Chief Of Staff to the First Lady)
7. $84,000 - Lelyveld, Catherine M. (Director and Press Secretary to the First Lady)
8. $75,000 - Starkey, Frances M. (Director of Scheduling and Advance for the First Lady)
9. $70,000 - Sanders, Trooper (Deputy Director of Policy and Projects for the First Lady)

10. $65,000 - Burnough, Erinn J. (Deputy Director and Deputy Social Secretary)
11. $64,000 - Reinstein, Joseph B. (Deputy Director and Deputy Social Secretary)
12. $62,000 - Goodman, Jennifer R. (Deputy Director of Scheduling and Events Coordinator For The First Lady)
13. $60,000 - Fitts, Alan O. (Deputy Director of Advance and Trip Director for the First Lady)
14. $57,500 - Lewis, Dana M. (Special Assistant and Personal Aide to the First Lady)
15. $52,500 - Mustaphi, Semonti M. (Associate Director and Deputy Press Secretary to The First Lady)
16. $50,000 - Jarvis, Kristen E. (Special-2Assistant for Scheduling and Traveling Aide to The First Lady)
17. $45,000 - Lechtenberg, Tyler A. (Associate Director of Correspondence For The First Lady)
18. $43,000 - Tubman, Samantha (Deputy Associate Director, Social Office)
19. $40,000 - Boswell, Joseph J. (Executive Assistant to the Chief Of Staff to the First Lady)
20. $36,000 - Armbruster, Sally M. (Staff Assistant to the Social Secretary)
21. $35,000 - Bookey, Natalie (Staff Assistant)
22. $35,000 - Jackson, Deilia A. (Deputy Associate Director of Correspondence for the First Lady)(This is community organizing at it's finest.)

There has NEVER been anyone in the White House at any time who has created such an army of staffers whose sole duties are the facilitation of the First Lady's social life. One wonders why she needs so much help, at taxpayer expense, when even Hillary, only had three; Jackie Kennedy one; Laura Bush one; and prior to Mamie Eisenhower social help came from the President's own pocket.

Note: This does not include makeup artist Ingrid Grimes-Miles, 49, and "First Hairstylist" Johnny Wright, 31, both of whom traveled aboard Air Force One to Europe.

FRIENDS.....THESE SALARIES ADD UP TO SIX MILLION, THREE HUNDRED SIXTY FOUR THOUSAND DOLLARS ($6,364,000) FOR THE 4 YEARS OF OFFICE?????   AND WE ARE IN A RECESSION????? WELL....MOST OF US ARE. I GUESS IT'S OK TO SPEND WILDLY WHEN IT'S NOT YOUR OWN MONEY?????

The Fix

There recently was an article in the St. Petersburg , Fl. Times. The Business Section asked readers for ideas on: "How Would You Fix the Economy?" I think this guy nailed it!

Dear Mr. President,

Please find below my suggestion for fixing America 's economy. Instead of giving billions of dollars to companies that will squander the money on lavish parties and unearned bonuses, use the following plan. You can call it the "Patriotic Retirement Plan":

There are about 40 million people over 50 in the work force. Pay them $1 million apiece severance for early retirement with the following stipulations:

1) They MUST retire. Forty million job openings - Unemployment fixed.

2) They MUST buy a new AMERICAN Car. Forty million cars ordered - Auto Industry fixed.

3) They MUST either buy a house or pay off their mortgage - Housing Crisis fixed.

It can't get any easier than that!!

P.S. If more money is needed, have all members in

Ron Berger   243

Congress pay their taxes...

Mr. President, while you're at it, make Congress retire on Social Security and Medicare. I'll bet both programs would be fixed pronto!

Actually that sounds like a doable solution. More thought needs to be invested, but it sure looks like a win-win situation.

Other points of view from one of our fore-fathers:

I thought this was very interesting and you might enjoy,

Thomas Jefferson was a very remarkable man who started learning very early in life and never stopped.

At 5, began studying under his cousins tutor.

At 9, studied Latin, Greek and French.

At 14, studied classical literature and additional languages.

At 16, entered the College of William and Mary.

At 19, studied Law for 5 years starting under George Wythe.

At 23, started his own law practice.

At 25, was elected to the Virginia House of Burgesses.

At 31, wrote the widely circulated "Summary View of the Rights of British America" and retired from his law practice.

At 32, was a Delegate to the Second Continental Congress.

At 33, wrote the Declaration of Independence.

At 33, took three years to revise Virginia 's legal code and wrote a Public Education bill and a statute for Religious Freedom.

At 36, was elected the second Governor of Virginia succeeding Patrick Henry.

At 40, served in Congress for two years.

At 41, was the American minister to France and negotiated commercial treaties with European nations along with Ben Franklin and John Adams.

At 46, served as the first Secretary of State under George Washington.

At 53, served as Vice President and was elected president of the American Philosophical Society.

At 55, drafted the Kentucky Resolutions and became the active head of Republican Party.

At 57, was elected the third president of the United States .

At 60, obtained the Louisiana Purchase doubling the nation's size.

At 61, was elected to a second term as President.

At 65, retired to Monticello .

At 80, helped President Monroe shape the Monroe Doctrine.

At 81, almost single-handedly created the University of Virginia and served as its first president.

At 83, died on the 50th anniversary of the Signing of the Declaration of Independence along with John Adams

Thomas Jefferson knew because he-himself studied the previous failed attempts at government. He understood actual history, the nature of God, his laws and the nature of man. That happens to be way more than what most understand today. Jefferson really knew his stuff. A voice from the past to lead us in the future:

John F. Kennedy held a dinner in the white House for a group of the brightest minds in the nation at that time. He made this statement:"This is perhaps the assembly of the most intelligence ever to gather at one time in the White House with the exception of when Thomas Jefferson dined alone."

When we get piled upon one another in large cities, as in Europe, we shall become as corrupt as Europe.
Thomas Jefferson

The democracy will cease to exist when you take away from those who are willing to work and give to those who would not.
Thomas Jefferson

It is incumbent on every generation to pay its own debts as it goes. A principle which if acted on would save one-half the wars of the world.
Thomas Jefferson

I predict future happiness for Americans if they can prevent the government from wasting the labors of the people under the pretense of taking care of them.
Thomas Jefferson

My reading of history convinces me that most bad government results from too much government.
Thomas Jefferson

No free man shall ever be debarred the use of arms.
  Thomas Jefferson

The   strongest reason for the people to retain the right to keep and bear arms is, as a last   resort, to protect themselves against tyranny in government.
  Thomas Jefferson

The tree of   liberty must be refreshed from time to time with the blood of patriots and tyrants.
  Thomas Jefferson

To compel a   man to subsidize with his taxes the propagation   of ideas which he disbelieves and abhors is sinful and tyrannical.
  Thomas Jefferson

Thomas Jefferson said in 1802:

I believe that   banking institutions are more dangerous to our   liberties than standing armies. If the   American people ever allow private banks to control the issue of their currency, first   by inflation, then by deflation, the banks and corporations that will grow up around the banks will deprive the people of all   property - until their children wake-up homeless on the continent their fathers conquered.

Here's another suggestion:

Hire Wal-Mart to Run the Government

1. Americans spend $36,000,000 at Wal-Mart every hour of every day.

2. This works out to $20,928 profit every minute!

3. Wal-Mart will sell more from January 1 to St. Patrick's Day (March 17th) than Target sells all year.

4. Wal-Mart is bigger than Home Depot + Kroger + Target +Sears + Costco + K-Mart combined.

5. Wal-Mart employs 1.6 million people, is the world's largest private employer, and most speak English.

6. Wal-Mart is the largest company in the history of the world.

7. Wal-Mart now sells more food than Kroger and Safeway combined, and keep in mind they did this in only fifteen years.

8. During this same period, 31 big supermarket chains sought bankruptcy.

9. Wal-Mart now sells more food than any other store in the world.

10. Wal-Mart has approx 3,900 stores in the USA of which 1,906 are Super Centers; this is 1,000 more than it had five years ago.

11. This year 7.2 billion different purchasing experiences will occur at Wal-Mart stores. (Earth's population is approximately 6.5 Billion.)

12. 90% of all Americans live within fifteen miles of a Wal-Mart.

You may think that I am complaining, but I am really laying the ground work for suggesting that MAYBE we should hire the guys who run Wal-Mart to fix the economy.

This should be read and understood by all Americans Democrats, Republicans, EVERYONE!!

To President Obama and all 535 voting members of the Congress,

It is now official you are ALL corrupt morons:

a. The U.S. Postal Service was established in 1775. You have had 234 years to get it right and it is broke.

b. Social Security was established in 1935. You have had 74 years to get it right and it is broke.

c. Fannie Mae was established in 1938. You have had 71 years to get it right and it is broke.

d. War on Poverty started in 1964. You have had 45 years to get it right; $1 trillion of our money is confiscated each year and transferred to "the poor" and they only want more.

e. Medicare and Medicaid were established in 1965. You have had 44 years to get it right and they are broke.

f. Freddie Mac was established in 1970. You have had 39 years to get it right and it is broke.

g. The Department of Energy was created in 1977 to lessen our dependence on foreign oil. It has ballooned to 16,000 employees with a budget of $24 billion a year and we import more oil than ever before. You had 32 years to get it right and it is an abysmal failure.

You have FAILED in every "government service" you have shoved down our throats while overspending our tax dollars.

AND YOU WANT AMERICANS TO BELIEVE YOU CAN BE TRUSTED WITH A GOVERNMENT-RUN HEALTH CARE SYSTEM ??

MAYBE WE OUGHT TO KICK OBAMA AND YOUR EGG-HEAD BUDDY BUMS OUT OF OFFICE AND HIRE WAL-MART TO RUN THE GOVERNMENT ???

WAL-MART SEEMS TO KNOW HOW TO RUN A BUSINESS.......WHY DON'T YOU GUYS JUST ADMIT IT'S WAY BEYOND YOUR PAY GRADE, AND QUIT?

One last suggestion and one that needs to be done first:

THIS IS HOW YOU FIX CONGRESS AND THE SENATE!

I am sending this to many and that includes conservatives, liberals, and everybody in between. Even though we disagree on a number of issues, I count all of you as friends.. My friend and neighbor wants to promote a "Congressional Reform Act of 2010". It would contain eight provisions, all of which would probably be strongly endorsed by those who drafted the Constitution and the Bill of Rights.

I know many of you will say, "this is impossible". Let me remind you, Congress has the lowest approval of any entity in Government, now is the time when Americans will join together to reform Congress - the entity that represents us.

We need to get a Senator to introduce this bill in the US Senate and a Representative to introduce a similar bill in the US House. These people will become American hero's..

Thanks,
A Fellow American

Congressional Reform Act of 2010

1. Term Limits: 12 years only, one of the possible options below.

A. Two Six year Senate terms
B. Six Two year House terms
C. One Six year Senate term and three Two Year House terms

Serving in Congress is an honor, not a career. The Founding Fathers envisioned citizen legislators, serve your term(s), then go home and back to work.

2. No Tenure / No Pension:

A congressman collects a salary while in office and receives no pay when they are out of office.

Serving in Congress is an honor, not a career. The Founding Fathers envisioned citizen legislators, serve your term(s), then go home and back to work.

3. Congress (past, present & future) participates in Social Security:

All funds in the Congressional retirement fund moves to the Social Security system immediately. All future funds flow into the Social Security system, Congress participates with the American people.

Serving in Congress is an honor, not a career. The Founding Fathers envisioned citizen legislators, server your term(s), then go home and back to work.

4. Congress can purchase their own retirement plan just as all Americans.

Serving in Congress is an honor, not a career. The Founding Fathers envisioned citizen legislators, serve your term(s), then go home and back to work.

5. Congress will no longer vote themselves a pay raise. Congressional pay will rise by the lower of CPI or 3%.

Serving in Congress is an honor, not a career. The Founding Fathers envisioned citizen legislators, serve your term(s), then go home and back to work.

6. Congress loses their current health care system and participates in the same health care system as the American people.

Serving in Congress is an honor, not a career. The Founding Fathers envisioned citizen legislators, serve your term(s), then go home and back to work.

7. Congress must equally abide in all laws they impose on the American people.

Serving in Congress is an honor, not a career. The Founding Fathers envisioned citizen legislators, serve your term(s), then go home and back to work.

8. All contracts with past and present congressmen are void effective 1/1/11.

The American people did not make this contract with congressmen, congressmen made all these contracts for themselves.

Serving in Congress is an honor, not a career.. The Founding Fathers envisioned   citizen legislators, serve your term(s), then go home and back to work.

I PLEDGE ALLEGIANCE TO THE FLAG,

OF THE UNITED STATES OF AMERICA ,

AND TO THE REPUBLIC FOR WHICH IT

STANDS, ONE NATION UNDER GOD,

INDIVISIBLE, WITH LIBERTY AND

JUSTICE FOR ALL!

If Muslims can pray on Madison Avenue, why are Christians banned from praying in public and erecting religious displays on their holy days?

It is said that 86% of Americans believe in God.

Therefore I have a very hard time understanding why there is such a problem in having 'In God! We Trust' on our money and having 'God' in the Pledge of Allegiance.

I believe it's time we stand up for what we believe!

One more thing before I quit:

19 Facts About The Deindustrialization Of America That Will Blow Your Mind The United States is rapidly becoming the very first "post-industrial" nation on the globe. All great economic empires eventually become fat and lazy and squander the great wealth that their forefathers have left them, but the pace at which America is accomplishing this is absolutely amazing.

It was America that was at the forefront of the industrial revolution. It was America that showed the world how to mass produce everything from automobiles to televisions to airplanes. It was the great American manufacturing base that crushed

Germany and Japan in World War II. But now we are witnessing the deindustrialization of America .

Tens of thousands of factories have left the United States in the past decade alone. Millions upon millions of manufacturing jobs have been lost in the same time period. The United States has become a nation that consumes everything in sight and yet produces increasingly little. Do you know what our biggest export is today? Waste paper. Yes, trash is the number one thing that we ship out to the rest of the world as we voraciously blow our money on whatever the rest of the world wants to sell to us.

The United States has become bloated and spoiled and our economy is now   just a shadow of what it once was.   Once upon a time America could literally out produce the rest of the world combined.   Today that is no longer true, but Americans sure do consume more than anyone else in the world.   If the deindustrialization of America continues at this current pace, what possible kind of a future are we going to be leaving to our children? Any great nation throughout history has been great at making things. So if the United States continues to allow its manufacturing base to erode at a staggering pace how in the world can the U.S. continue to consider itself to be a great nation?

We have created the biggest debt bubble in the history of the world in an effort to maintain a very high standard of living, but the current state of affairs is not anywhere close to sustainable. Every single month America goes into more debt and every single month America gets poorer.

So what happens when the debt bubble pops? The deindustrialization of the United States should be a top concern for every man, woman and child in the country. But sadly, most Americans do not have any idea what is going on around them . For people like that, take this article and print it out and hand it to them. Perhaps what they will read below will shock them badly enough to awaken them from their slumber. The following are 19 facts about the deindustrialization of America that will blow your mind....

#1 The United States has lost approximately 42,400 factories since 2001. About 75 percent of those factories employed over 500 people when they were still in operation.

#2 Dell Inc., one of America 's largest manufacturers of computers, has announced plans to dramatically expand its operations in China with an investment of over $100 billion over the next decade.

#3 Dell has announced that it will be closing its last large U.S. manufacturing facility in Winston-Salem , North Carolina in November. Approximately 900 jobs will be lost.

#4 In 2008, 1.2 billion cell phones were sold worldwide. So how many of them were manufactured inside the United States ? Zero.

#5 According to a new study conducted by the Economic Policy Institute, if the U.S. trade deficit with China continues to increase at its current rate, the U.S. economy will lose over half a million jobs this year alone.

#6 As of the end of July, the U.S. trade deficit with China had risen 18 percent compared to the same time period a year ago.

#7 The United States has lost a total of about 5.5 million manufacturing jobs since October 2000.

#8 According to Tax Notes, between 1999 and 2008 employment at the foreign affiliates of U.S. parent companies increased an astounding 30 percent to 10.1 million. During that exact same time period, U.S. employment at American multinational corporations declined 8 percent to 21.1 million.

#9 In 1959, manufacturing represented 28 percent of U.S. economic output. In 2008, it represented 11.5 percent.

#10 Ford Motor Company recently announced the closure of a factory that produces the Ford Ranger in

St. Paul , Minnesota . Approximately 750 good paying middle class jobs are going to be lost because making Ford Rangers in Minnesota does not fit in with Ford's new "global" manufacturing strategy.

#11 As of the end of 2009, less than 12 million Americans worked in manufacturing. The last time less than 12 million Americans were employed in manufacturing was in 1941.

#12 In the United States today, consumption accounts for 70 percent of GDP. Of this 70 percent, over half is spent on services.

#13 The United States has lost a whopping 32 percent of its manufacturing jobs since the year 2000.

#14 In 2001, the United States ranked fourth in the world in per capita broadband Internet use. Today it ranks 15th.

#15 Manufacturing employment in the U.S. computer industry is actually lower in 2010 than it was in 1975.

#16 Printed circuit boards are used in tens of thousands of different products. Asia now produces 84 percent of them worldwide.

#17 The United States spends approximately $3.90 on Chinese goods for every $1 that the Chinese spend on goods from the United States .

#18 One prominent economist is projecting that the Chinese economy will be three times larger than the U.S. economy by the year 2040.

#19 The U.S. Census Bureau says that 43.6 million Americans are now living in poverty and according to them that is the highest number of poor Americans in the 51 years that records have been kept.

So how many tens of thousands more factories do we need to lose before we do something about it? How many millions more Americans are going to become unemployed before we all admit that we have a very, very serious problem on our hands? How many more trillions of dollars are going to leave the country before we realize that we are losing wealth at a pace that is killing our economy?

How many once great manufacturing cities are going to become rotting war zones like Detroit before we understand that we are committing national economic suicide? The deindustrialization of America is a national crisis. It needs to be treated like one. America is in deep, deep trouble folks. It is time to wake up!

--

~~~~~~~~~~~~~~~~~~~~~~

Columbia College records -- Not released
Columbia thesis -- Not released
Harvard College records -- Not released
Harvard Law Review articles -- None Signed
Original birth certificate -- Not released
Baptism certificate -- None
Medical records -- Not released
Illinois State Senate records -- None (Locked up to prohibit public view)
Illinois State Senate schedule -- Lost (All other Illinois state senators' records are intact)
Nothing wrong here! Move on.

THE NOSE ON YOUR FACE.COM

Post Script

You may have noticed that I use numerous emails that have been sent to me in a number of my books. I do this because they seem to be so well written that I couldn't improve on them if I tried.

Some you may have received yourself. Most are "public domain" and others I've received permission to publish. The trouble with receiving these emails the normal way is that one by one they don't seem so important. However, when you group them together you'll realize that we're in a heap of trouble.

I, for the life of me, cannot see the "good" in BO. He has lied and hidden his claims so that no one can verify what he's saying. There is only one in a billion chance that his reasoning is good. He doesn't even know how many States we have in our Union.

I fear for our country, even though I hope I'm wrong. I do not want my children or my grandchildren to say that my generation had a chance to do something and didn't. I am just one lone voice in the wilderness trying to bring forth the truth, as I know it, and help redirect this country back to our roots. BO may be a good speaker, but what he says doesn't seem to arouse a suspicious press like political BS used to. There used to be "investigative" reporters that loved to dig and dig until a juicy story was found.

We have suffered through bad Presidents before, but none of them were bent on turning the country into a Socialistic Third World has been in four years.

The only way to revive this country is to send in new blood in November 2012. Not the same old tired blood that's been around for years, but brand new blood to rejuvenate our land.

We also need to pray unceasing that the Good Lord will help us rid the demons and allow us to bring back our values. Not only is the Constitution needed to be brought back in the light, but also the Bible. This country was founded on Christian/Judea principles and those opposing it need to sit quietly and listen.

* * WARNING * *

IF YOU LET THE "TEA PARTY FLAME" GO OUT AND YOU PREFER A TIRED "HAS BEEN" FROM THE PAST TO LEAD YOU IN 2012 - BO WILL WIN A 2ND TERM AND THE COUNTRY WILL BE DOOMED. THEN I CAN ONLY SAY . . .

May God have mercy on our Souls

www.ingramcontent.com/pod-product-compliance
Lightning Source LLC
Chambersburg PA
CBHW060839280326
41934CB00007B/849